Dedicated to my mother
Lady H. Ejiogu (KSJ)

Chinwendu H. Ugwezuoha, *my sister*
who opened the spirituality of women to me

Vera Ejiogu, *my daughter*
who manifests the diaspora spirituality
of an African lady

Margot de Zeeuw
who helped awaken my African spirituality
during my theology study

Matty Njie
who manifests the African women's
authority in her lifestyle

Fester Odion Imoh
who is a role model in African women's
education & leadership

&

All African Women
and women protecting life & wellbeing

*Where the battle is the fiercest, God places
his best army. Women do not battle with
man-made weapons.*

*When God wants to change the course of history,
He shifts the man away and works with women.*

*This is the motto of this book.
A motto that is at the core of African spirituality,
but also at the core of Biblical spirituality.*

RECOMMENDATIONS

Breaking Life-threatening Taboos
In the circle of life

Godian takes us with him in the meeting of a group of African women. It started with a phone call from one woman, to come and help. You understand immediately how there was a seed of trust planted a long time ago in their contact.

This phone call Godian answered by coming, listening, and understanding at the place where a group of women comes together. By storytelling, he tells about the women and their lives by mentioning them with names, telling their stories and all kind of aspects of their (hard) life.

In the stories, you learn also about nature, birth community, the thinking of good, God, taboos, and power. So, you can discover the warm heart center and surrounding of African thinking, best worded as "thinking in the round". Godian built a strong community with the women, where they can help each other and learn from each other, from within their own sources.

Godian invites us to learn about this wealth of African life (Important to read in the mirror of his efforts to learn about Dutch society, culture, and people). It is important for everyone who meets people with African roots, especially professionals to learn deeply about the aspects of life, where are the taboos, where you misunderstand, can hurt, but more, where you can help flourish people, to help them use their sources and overcome their barriers and traumas and strengthen the power and live energy.

I will recommend this book, as a travel guide through living with people with African roots, and for professionals who work with them.

I am grateful for the gift of this book and the richness of African thinking in the round. The connectedness with nature, the rivers, the land, and the inclusion power of African living and thinking. It gives us so much richness to rethink and renew our practice with nature, with our spirituality in connection with others and nature in reciprocity, in the circle of life.

Marchien Timmerman, MA, Theology, Lecturer & team leader
University of Applied Science, Theology and Worldview in Windesheim.

RECOMMENDATIONS

vii

Women's Natural Authority

Since I meet Godian Ejiogu, I have always seen him as a rare gene. This book written by a man that portrays the soul and heart of African women is rare to find. It is rare to find a man who is committed to women's affairs like Godian is. The confidentiality the women have in him, to trust their hearts to him is rare. Godian did not disappoint but presented them and their stories with examples that made this difficult and deep spirituality accessible to outsiders.

As an African woman, he showed why we are not threatened by men. He showed why we are not struggling with emancipation in men's world. This is because we know our authority and how to use it. We know our women's world, responsibility, place, and men know their own place. We know who we are and how to maintain equilibrium in life and creation.

Godian portrays how African women apply their authority in order not to threaten the men or make them lose their identity which can lead to an identity crisis. African women let the men do their things until it is clear to them that it is not working, or until they are endangering life that women hold precious. Women will direct the situation for life protection.

In our world full of confusion and lack of clear direction to living in joy and peace, this book is a guide. In a world where men and women are entangled in a struggle for power and position, women can understand that they are imbued with a gift different from men. Men should recognize women's gifts.

This book is for every woman and every man. It is for a society seeking joy and peaceful coexistence both in gender and cultural issues of life. I, therefore, recommend it for all policymakers and all human beings both Africans and non-Africans.

I thank Godian for travelling with women and sharing these pearls and diamonds with us. I also thank the women who had such durable trust and confidence in Godian and shared this deep richness with the world.

Matty Njie, BSC in international communication management,
(helping people to understand each other and cooperate)

RECOMMENDATIONS

LIVING IN A GLOBAL WORLD

Keeping in mind the great cultural diversity of peoples on the African continent, this book is a helpful introduction for westerners like me to get a better understanding of the spiritual and social values that are deeply appreciated by African communities, and how these values influence social relations and offer a source of spiritual strength and mental resilience. The book shows the richness that African cultures have to offer, both to present-day African societies and to over-individualised western societies where Africans may be living in diaspora. It also sheds some light on the issues of cultural sensitivity, diversity, stress, and other tensions arising from multicultural societies and multireligious societies. The book helps to better understand why the lack of a cultural approach affects the health of African migrants.

Global transformations since the Second World War have been huge and fast, and have been affecting all societies. I hope readers will value this book as a starting point to rethink our common futures, and what is needed to be able to nurture the best of both worlds. Let our thoughts be provoked on the reconfiguration of our societies and relationships between African and western peoples, both in diaspora in western countries and on a global level.

Madelon Grant, MA Religious studies

WHOLENESS

This is a book of paradoxes: Taboos around the mental health of African women must remain unveiled, yet there is a need to talk about it. Vulnerability and power are not mutually exclusive. Culturally specific concepts are recognizable for non-Africans.

An extremely important book with the power to strengthen wholeness in us all.

Elly Rijnierse, MA Political Science.

RECOMMENDATIONS

A SPIRITUAL CAREGIVER

In Resilent African Women, spiritual caregive Godian Ejiogu takes as a starting point the problems African women are facing in Rotterdam's health care system. They tell things that health care providers here in our time are not used to hear. Ejiogu chooses to tell the stories of those women and provide a sketch of the philosophy of life and culture of African people behind them. Ejiogu shows that African people hold a philosophy of life and culture in which the family and community are central to connecting with ancestors, spirits and God through leaders and rituals. It seems an impossible task to describe the roots of the people of such a vast continent, including those who were enslaved and those who migrated here. Yet Ejiogu manage doing precisely this. His own background as a man from the great IBO tribe in Nigeria emerges from that description as well as his Catholic background.

This book can only do its job well if it provokes discussion and is not seen as a dogmatics of African philosophy of life. There are too many things that call for change such as the removal of the clitoris in women's initiation, the taboo of abortion and euthanasia, the blind spot for the uniqueness of gays, lesbians and others. Ejiogu, as if he were a reporter, shows the good and bad sides of African communual thinking without judgment and without giving his opinion. That is precisely what makes the book interesting as an introduction to African philosophy of life for spiritual caregivers in particular and caregivers in general.

Freda Dröes, spiritual caregiver

AFRICAN WOMEN

ISBN: 978-90-79516-08-7 - *hardcover*
ISBN: 978-90-79516-09-4 - *e-book*

Published by
Peace Servant - peaceservant.nl

Design & Production
Tim B. Gilman | timmyroland.com

RESPONSIBILITY
The author is responsible for the contents of this book. He offers training, education, presentations, workshops and personal support to individuals and groups upon invitation. Contact via: minister@ peaceservant.nl

TABLE OF CONTENTS

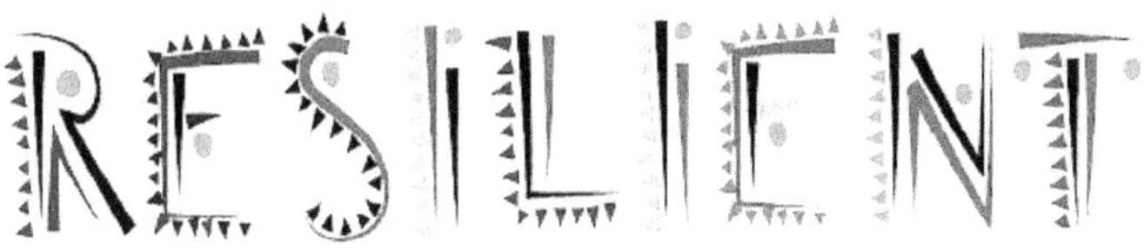

AFRICAN WOMEN

Godian Ejiogu

RESILIENT
AFRICAN WOMEN

Chapter 1

A PHONE CALL FOR HELP

'Come and help us, please!' I heard the caller's voice say when I picked up an incoming phone call. I recognized the voice. I know the person by name and face. I worked with her almost a decade ago. I am her confidant. She continued, 'we are dying here, and nobody understands us. It is too much for us and no one cares. We need your help!'

This was in April 2020. The corona pandemic popularly known as COVID-19 had only been present in the Netherlands for about two months. The intensity of the fear and anxiety transmitted through the voice sent chills down my spine. She narrated the story of people dying in old people's homes. I know the old people's home, I used to celebrate a service there every other month, and I gave spiritual care to the inhabitants. My last liturgical service before I left the city ten years ago was in that home. I quickly felt connected again to the suffering of the people as she narrated it to me. Many migrants are living there, and many have died already.

She went on to narrate other home violence both men and women were going through. Women burned all over their bodies. Some cannot sit or lie down because of the open wounds kneeling or standing were the less painful positions. They were clothed in long robes to allow their wounds to air out. Tight clothes that touch the skin would stick to the fresh bleeding wounds making healing difficult, and they have to heal quickly. Anything that helped was applied to make sure they could sit or lie down within a few days. There was no further medical treatment from the specialist, and there was no more money to buy extra first-aid materials to treat them. The victims have no safe place for shelter, and there is no one to care for them except for their companions who participate in their suffering. They could not go to the police for fear of the safety of their family. They could not inform official institutions due to the lack of trust. They want to avoid more troubles for their family and relationships. They prefer to suffer alone than to let the whole family and community suffer with them. Some men had the same reactions and suffered in the same way.

She continued with the stories of those who are suffering similarly in their homes. Families who are crowded living in small spaces, people who are mentally disoriented, the tears and frustrations of old people who can not see their families, and the frustration of people who can not go out to socialize and see others, just to get out of the house for a few hours.

Poverty and hunger were on the list. People have nothing to eat, they are locked in their homes, and nobody knows how they are doing. They have no savings to buy food. They could not make phone calls because they do not have the money to buy cards to make calls. They could not go out to ask for help from the network they have. Gatherings and social contacts were forbidden. While the list continued, my mind was racing on how to answer the call to come over and help. I listened to her and comforted her, but also encouraged her to keep up the great work. I told her that I will call her back. She added, 'please come, and help us, nobody is helping us here. We are dying.' We hung up. Her last words kept echoing in my mind.

In the past, I was involved in the Amsterdam Southeast social issues intervention. In 2012, I had the same kind of request as the one above. During my work as a spiritual caregiver for drug and alcohol users in the city of Amsterdam, a lady I knew since 1993 approached me and told me about the plight of Africans in Amsterdam. She ended her long story with a desperate request, 'come and help us, we do not have any future outlook, and neither do our children'. For a genuine reason known only to me, I immediately refuted the request and left. However, her desperate voice and request kept on echoing in my mind and I decided to look into it. I was soon convinced that I should heed the call. I later stopped my work for drugs and alcohol users and went to intervene in the social, economic, spiritual and mental health and general condition of the Africans and people with African roots in Amsterdam Southeast. It was then that I learned how Amsterdam Southeast was a hub of the scarcity of basic things for life but it also has an abundance of inconveniences against health and well-being for Africans in the Netherlands. For example, this was the first place in the Netherlands where the former minister for Defense, Bijleveld-Schouten sent food support to alleviate the poverty and hunger among the inhabitants during the COVID-19 pandemic. These food packages had been stored by the ministry for the Dutch military for training and camps in foreign countries but these foreign missions were postponed due to COVID-19 and that is why the food was available to be distributed. Amsterdam Southeast received this with joy and there was a big mobilization in this region to support and serve the communities of migrants living there.

So, after rationally dissecting the situation, I felt freer to investigate the call for help in the city of Rotterdam. There is attention for the migrants in Amsterdam Southeast already, but the migrant community in another city was facing a silent disaster. It was clear to me that the call to come meant trust and it was desperately needed. As a migrant from African roots, I could understand the urgency of the call and why they are in such situation. I had seen it all and experienced it all in many levels of the society.

RETURN CALL

After four days, I called her back because I needed some time to see if I had anything to offer them. However, the topic of the return call was not only the present issue. I wanted to know more about why there is no help for them, why there is nobody left taking care of them, why were they not understood, and why they were so isolated. I left the city after my work there was finished ten years ago, and I had so many questions. After her response, I felt it was time for me to go back to work there again.

VISIT

When I visited to ascertain the situation, the reality I met was even more troubling than I originally thought. People who were suffering domestic violence, had nowhere to seek temporary shelter, others had all different kinds of health challenges that were not being taken care of. After I left there that day, I knew I was in for a lot of work. I understood well that Africans are currently facing the most difficult situation in the country. I learned this during my research in 1996. It is understandable why they lose trust in institutions and other organizations in society except for what they themselves can do. I understand why they are in such a situation without basic help. Because of this, I felt I had no choice other than to be part of the solution.

The plan I constructed to help them went into effect after all the COVID- 19 measures were abolished. While these safety measures were still in place, I stood with them online with support, prayer, training, education, tutoring, counseling, and coaching. In February 2022 we started gathering socially in person, and this was the birth of the content of this book. In physical gatherings, you can build more trust than online. Above all, many of the people involved could not manage online communication well. Almost all of them have no privacy at home to talk about the issues bothering them. Some women were sharing apartments, whereby each mother would take one room to share with her children. Such mothers could not share with outsiders what life is like in that home in the presence of other family members. It is like betrayal, especially of trust, privacy, and autonomy. Nobody in the family will feel safe with that person.

"Please tell society about us" was the unanimous request of all the women in the group.

When I asked them to come and share their story with society, they all refused. So, I am the one tasked to tell society about them. The organizations involved in this community have gathered about 2500 women in one city and I spoke with many of the members. Here, I will present at least a few names. Outside this specific organization, I also worked with many other African organizations and leaders of organizations. The number of people covered by those organizations was seven thousand people with African roots. The leaders, who were mostly men, and some are spiritual leaders or chaplains, maintained the confidentiality of my talk with them. This is because men strictly do not want to talk about the topic. But these leaders told me how they will be pleased if I can tell the stories.

I realized that after hearing them and seeing them, keeping it secret would be ethically and morally incorrect. As I long to hear them, I also long to tell their stories. So, I thought about it and decided to share these stories in this book. With it, I hope to contribute to the understanding that we are all born and brought up in a culture. A culture that is a barrier but can also be a uniting source. I hope the readers of the book will create a spiritual space in themselves to accept the invitation given by this book and enter the world of these African roots. Some of them their ancestors left African continents more than three centuries ago. They themselves had not been to Africa. Some just arrived from Africa less than a decade ago. This book shows what make them still African roots in The Netherlands.

In the last three decades of my involvement working and living in a multicultural setting in the Netherlands, cultural sensitivity has become something I do not take lightly. In the last decade, there has been little attention paid to cultural sensitivity, competence, and so on. With the women, we looked into their cultural background to help them see where the conflicts with their present society and culture lie. We searched together for a healthy approach of how to live their lives within the present culture, and we had insightful moments by recalling their culture of origin. This is easier because the majority of those involved were first-generation migrants who have immigrant families in the country.

Because they still vividly remember the culture of their birth and the initiations they went through, they were able to draw sharp differences between their culture and the culture of their new country. The awareness of the culture of their new country, in contrast with the culture of their birth, clarified to them that their present approach to their current problems will not work. They need the culture of their new country to break through in solving their problems. With this knowledge, they decided to break the taboos. At the same time, they know that breaking the taboos is not the only step towards tackling the problems, they cannot succeed without support. They have their limitations as is normally known in the community. The first and most important step is to talk. The next step is to open up.

This book is meant to fulfill the second step. To open, one needs a listening ear without prejudice. Above all a level of understanding is needed for one to continue his or her story. This book hopes to open the minds of those who are supposed to at least understand the story and situation of this migrant's roots. It is another culture and continent, but a human culture and human life.

HEALTH TABOOS

NAMING THE SPIRITS

I arrived a few minutes before the starting time. The women had gathered already and were waiting for me. I was surprised that they came so early. There were dozens of them. They had fearful expressions on their faces, they looked worried, and some even looked desperate. The door was open because of the hot summer in July 2022. It was still morning hours. We were facing a heat wave, which means the day and night temperatures had been high for many consecutive days. I was briefly introduced by their leader to those who did not know me. I was invited by her to inform them on the reason of the gathering even though I was actually expecting her to tell me why they invited me to come and help them break the taboos. It turned out that I was the one to tell them why they should come together to break the taboos. I had actually already spoken to many of them in personal consultations. I know their stories and I know they are community-shared experiences. I know the anxiety they are facing and I know the poverty and social challenges they are suffering because of their health problems. They are becoming conscious of the spiritual and mental effects of the taboos that have blocked their life and their living.

They were unable to move forward, and they did not know what to do. I was also somehow unable to move forward in helping them without them having the courage to break through the taboos together. There were too many of them for a personal consultation and it would not be as effective as a group consultation. Sharing their story with each other in the community would liberate many and they would realize that they are not alone. Together, they would find a community solution, as it is African custom to deal with issues in the community. I knew that some women were determined to break the taboos, but also afraid to speak in the presence of others. When I mentioned the taboo of spiritual and mental health, some stood up and ran away through the open door. However, I expected this uneasy reaction because I knew the reluctance of Africans to speak openly about taboos. The people who leaped out of the room showed physical reactions I recognized. Therefore, I applied a high level of cultural sensitivity in communicating the topic to them. As I was born, nurtured, and brought up in African culture until my adult age, I also went through and experienced many rituals of passage, and I am very conversant with the taboos and sensitivities of the culture, so I know what they are going through.

In writing this book to share these stories, a level of sensitivity is applied to the cultural sensibility of African culture. This is necessary for Africans who will read it with the taboos in mind. There are issues or topics I will not touch here because of the same reason of sensitivity. One should not talk about certain secrets that are trusted to you, both by men and by spirit. In such issues, you should share it with the community that shares the understanding.

One who knows African culture will understand this sensibility in this writing and that this is inherent in the communication of the culture. Because it is an oral culture in all aspects, its sensitivity is non-negotiable. One cannot take written documents to amend the culture and thereby make the needed change. Giving an example of religion, African traditional religions are not written religions with books or holy books. Each community practices its own rituals differently and none of the rituals can be repeated elsewhere in the same way. Each ritual leader follows the directives of the spirit or of his own instinct. This example is applicable to almost all parts of the culture because it is not in writing anywhere, and this makes negotiation with different communities or tribes difficult. This makes African culture an issue of the heart and soul. It is in the heart and soul where one stores their culture and the body becomes the expression of it. There are so many taboos that exist within the culture and one of the taboos we encountered during our gatherings was the health taboo.

Taboos are not only meant to protect the individual, but also to protect the community and the tribes. It is a strong element in community cohesion. It strengthens the identity of the community and creates a place of belonging. The community that respects and shares the taboo is stronger together and stands out above others who do not have a cohesive cultural element. In my town, we have a taboo of not going to our stream one day in an eight-day block. Our week is made up of eight days in contrast to the European calendar which is made up of seven days. When it comes to taboos, we maintain the eight days. When it comes to the world calendar, we maintain the seven days. One of the eight days is reserved for the spirits to go and do what they want to do in the water. On that specific day, nobody should go and touch the river.

One is not even allowed to walk to a distance where the river can be seen. It is a day when the river rests, settles, and becomes peaceful. The spirits of the river will have their time to purify the river and the fish can enjoy the water without human disturbances It is taboo to go to the river on such days, except for those who are allowed to go and maintain the custom. Any action of a person or group that violates this rule is termed as sacrilege to the spirit and community. It is assumed that the spirit of the water will not only punish the person but the whole community where the water is and where the person comes from, and if it happens that the person is not from there, the community where the river custom is violated will take the responsibility to assure that the particular ritual of restoration is made.

Therefore, the community where the river custom is violated will take the responsibility to assure that the particular ritual of restoration is made. This kind of taboo remains a myth in the custom. Nobody can explain how it came to be and whether it can be changed without serious consequences for a person or the community. When the river dries up to a worrisome level, rituals are done for the spirit. After this, the river will come back to its normal level.

There are words that are taboos in the culture too. Some words you cannot use when it is dark and some you can use only during the day. There are certain words or languages one is not allowed to use. There are people who are permitted to use those words or languages. These persons (I try to avoid using individuals) are permitted to do this based on their role and service to the community. The priests and leaders of altars are allowed to use those specific words. It is assumed that others who were not allowed to use those words will harm themselves if they do. In that sense, such words are taboos to protect the individual who might use it. Some words and taboos are forbidden based on moral language use. They are words that can be used to speak to an adult, but not to a child. There are also words one can use in the presence of a child when speaking to an adult. Most of those words are based on their moral and ethical use of them.

SPIRIT

Naming a spirit or godhead, deities and God differs in Taboo. Some spirits can be named, and others cannot be named. This taboo is based on personal and community protection. It is believed that when you mention a name, the person you called is supposed to answer or show a sign that they heard you. This is in case the person is within hearing distance. In case they are not around, it is believed that calling that person's name distracts them from what they are doing. It does not matter how far away the person might be. When one's name is mentioned, the spirit of that person picks it up and responds. Culturally, when someone sneezes without a cold infection, it means somebody mentioned his name somewhere, either in discussion or remembrance.

Naming someone always has an effect on the person named. When the person is close, they will respond to their name. This is also applicable to spirits. When a spirit is mentioned or named, it comes to answer its name. When one mentions or calls on God, He will answer. When one mentions or calls on the ancestors, they are bound to answer. When one mentions or calls out the name of a wicked spirit, it will also come to answer its name. when you call what you do not want, or something that will bring a problem to you, then you are the one seeking such a problem. When one calls out to a wicked spirit, it is an invitation. Such an invitation can be an honor, or it can be for ritualistic reasons. Such wicked spirits can only be called by those who are authorized to do so. They will know how to handle them when they appear or respond. They also know how to call them so that they will not act disastrously. The necessary negotiation and courtesy in approaching such spirits are known by those professionals who are authorized to mediate with them. The professionals know how to master such spirits. They know how to praise it and give it more space and honor, or dishonor it and redeem the space it has taken. Such mastery is needed when working with them.

Others who are not authorized or who do not know the professional approach face taboo in mentioning the name. Although, Africa does not have the culture and mentality of mastering this. Her main culture is in expanding talent and using it. However, in certain cases that involve the spirit, mastering this is necessary because of the effect it has on the community that can easily lead to loss of lives and destruction of properties.

Mastering is the desire to contain and be in control, to master. It is known that mastering the devil or God or spirits is not reality. But having an approach based on communication and negotiation would prevent unnecessary damage and repair such damages that could be prevented. This is why taboo is laid on such areas of mentioning spirits, especially the wicked ones. A wicked spirit is one who inflicts sickness, hardship, and loss on people or communities. One has to be extremely careful with it.

Any time someone is sick or faces hazardous and painful issues, then it is assumed that a wicked spirit is at work with that person or community. Talking about health issues, both mental and physical health is broadcasting the effect the spirit has on the person. Such broadcasting is not only dangerous for the victim but also promotes the wicked spirit responsible for ill health.

This is also why Africans or black people want to avoid discussing voodoo, juju, and health issues relating to a spiritual health hazard. There are many other reasons, but it all comes down to the fear of the spirit and the surrounding people who might be involved in causing the problems. Exposing your problems means informing them how effectively their action works against you. It is like giving them credit for what they did. When such a spirit succeeds in its plan, it also means that either the victim is guilty or does not know how to counteract it. It makes one weaker and more vulnerable, and at the same time, it gives the actor more power. Health issues are correlated with spiritual things. Spiritual things are like your religion or faith. It is a private issue; you have to deal with your spiritual world.

This cultural thinking creates a barrier in communication and understanding with other cultures, especially when it comes to health issues. To break through the barrier in cultural communication, one needs to break some taboos that form the barriers. Africans do not have enough healthcare professionals who are culturally sensitive to their issues in order to attend to them. The consequence is that their health problem will increase and their quality of living will continue to deteriorate. Such a situation is what we want to shorten and probably prevent. We need to, therefore, go through the difficult and narrow road.

What the group proposed to me was challenging. I knew that everything relied on my approach to the situation. I saw many others who wanted to leave. The environment was charged. I was also not free to express certain forms of belief, for example, my Christian belief, because the majority were not Christians. There were probably also Muslims, Winti, Santeria, Afoxi / Candomblé / Umbanda, Wicca, Juju, Hoodoo, Voodoo, and so on, present there. They did not introduce themselves as being from the religions, this is my diagnosis based on their cultural background of birth, rituals they have undergone, expressions, and stories. I knew the meeting should yield a result that would make them continue to come together for more. It was the training I gave them on mental health that opened some of them up to me for a personal consultation, thereby giving me information to their personal struggles and loss attributed to the taboos.

I have learned in my years working with them, how important it is to take them by the hand. I also know when to leave their hand and let them go on their own. Especially when their inner strength is kindled, they can take up their life challenges in their own hands. They are highly gifted in handling their life affairs. I have to be patient until they are activated. To achieve that activation, I have to work on their perception of their reality. Creating a safe and trusted community where they can discuss health issues under my guidance is a basic goal of this meeting. Moreover, searching with them for the right cultural approach to their well-being is part of my interest because there was no prospect of moving further from where we currently were. I promised to help them because being stranded there and leaving them the way they were was not helping. I did know that the topic of mental health was taboo within African communities. Naming mental problems instill fear and dread in them because of the association with the suspected spirit involved.

The training period and personal consultation had given me more insight and shown me how much this African root needs separate guidance. Simply referring them to psychologists and psychiatrists is a step that many of them are not ready for. It is still a difficult group for mental health professionals, as they themselves noted during the training meetings where psychologists and other professionals in health fields participated. Even health professionals from the target group share the same fear of taboos. Their scientific health education did not prepare them for this aspect of health care. They think it is something for spiritual health professionals who are trained to talk about God, deity, and ancestor's spirit. This was one of the reasons I was stranded because referring them to psychologists and psychiatrists is not possible. It is neither safe for the professional nor for the patients, whose problems will become worse if the professional is insensitive to their calamity. At these meetings, professionals, and communities can meet and learn from each other. Only then can I talk about a safe referral.

I find it interesting to at least get closer to the core of their health problems and let them find the words to express it. Within the group are people who are highly traumatized, and depressed, anxiety is also a common disorder, as constant stress, and so on. They have a right to health care but that possibility is not there at the moment because they are not understood and cannot express themselves. I am concerned that dozens of people (and this number is growing all the time) who come to me currently can neither be referred to a medical health professional nor sent home without being given basic support.

I could not afford to fail in cementing a group that will succeed in taking care of themselves until professionals and institutions understand their situation and take responsibility for them. I was able to find the right things to say during my introduction for those who stayed. My introduction covered all forms of belief present and more, and with this, I noticed some of them relaxing. They were able to understand that I know what I am talking about. They understood that they are harming themselves by keeping and maintaining the taboos.

After my introduction, which contained elements that gave them the courage of safety, and authority, I invited them to speak up. I did not say any prayer out loud because they were from different religious backgrounds and continents represented. The only thing they had in common is that they have African roots, they have taboos, and they are all women and mothers. After long and insightful sharing and conversations with the participants, they were able to speak with confidence. Because the fear of spirits (God, deities, and ancestors) is very deeply rooted in the culture, it took a lot of time and effort to make it discussable. However, the participants recognized that these fears were holding them down, and for this very reason, they felt it was a significant step. According to them, this kind of gathering did not exist anywhere for people of African descent. Certainly, in the Netherlands, this approach does not exist.

However, they wanted to keep it absolutely secret and confidential. They experienced the relief they got and decided to meet at least every week. Every so, often, they met three times a week. I wanted to examine and break the taboos together with the participants carefully and cautiously. We did this in a culturally sensitive way. This was a great opportunity to address this persistent problem. As I expected, and as the participants also discovered, resolving the issue is a long process that requires patience and repetition. It is a culture deeply rooted in numerous issues.

As adults, it is also deeply rooted in them, and changing is difficult. They had to find a balance for their living and we were committed to it. The group remains only for those who participate in it. It can be extended, but not necessarily exposed to outsiders. I was authorized to share their story, but not for them to come and share it. I know in the future they will be kindled to summon the courage to take their story to outsiders and that will be evidence of liberation from the taboos.

RESILIENT

AFRICAN WOMEN

Chapter 3

HEALTH STORIES
& LINKS TO ILL HEALTH

This chapter is important to understand the rest of the book. The list of examples may seem long, but it makes it easier to understand the rest of the book. The spirits mentioned have different names in different languages. I left most of the names out. Each spirit has its own domain of residence and control. Places like forest, mountains, valleys, earth, water, air, but also family and community. They are spirits in charge of certain places and nature. Such belief is widely shared within African culture. That is why I would represent the places instead of mentioning the names of the spirit which could only represent a particular language community or zone.

I chose a few stories to share here as an illustration of the ones I heard. These stories are not unique to a specific person, but these are stories that are shared by different people who did not know each other. Most of them are represented in the stories. Even though they are from different nations and continents, they all have African roots. The names mentioned are for representation only and they do not represent countries or continents. It is important to note that men are not open to talking about the topic yet and it is remarkable that women have the courage to talk about it more than men. It is culture playing out. Women nurture life with their own life energy of blood, water, heart, mind, and soul. It makes them committed when it comes to saving life. African women have the resilience to handle issues that men could not handle.

Also, when a community have conflict with each other, marriage between both communities can bring the conflict to an end. One can think of many examples where women play the role of peace making between communities and nations. Think about war issues. The men will fight until they lose their sense in the war. They may not know how to stop or have the capacity to stop, but when women decide to end the war, it will end. When it comes to taboos and unsolvable problems in the community, women take it over by force from the men. Any issue in the hands of women is considered solved. This is what I knew as a child growing up in Africa. I, personally, witnessed countless incidents in my community where the women mobilized themselves, put the men aside, and solved years of life-threatening issues in just one day. It is striking to see it happening in Europe with African women.

It is a remarkable mark of respect seeing them take on these taboos like taking a bull by the horn. They asked me to share their stories for now because before they could not solve these life-threatening issues without the support of the responsible institutions and owners of the problems. If this country is their culture, they know what to do and how to solve the life threat to their well-being and their family. But unfortunately, it is not their culture. They, therefore, need institutions to take responsibility for the health care of all citizens. I will be concise in describing the stories they told. The meaning of the names given is added to show that African names have a meaning related to the person's vocation and biography.

The most dominating spirit mentioned was the Evil Eye. Almost all the women had a painful narration of how the Evil Eye had caused death in the family and health problems. Some suffered the loss of all their wealth, including businesses. Some even sold their house to carry out rituals to solve the problem. The effect of the Evil Eye in the life of their children was also shared by some of them. Some lost the life of their husband to the Evil Eye and some have children with mental problems because of the Evil Eye.

All spiritual, psychological, and mental disorders are associated with the spirit as the cause of them. All health problems are also associated with the spirit as the cause of it and most life challenges are linked to the spirit as the cause of it. In numerous instances, they still must go to the doctor just to see if they can get relief, but the hope is to go and settle with the particular spirit for total relief and freedom. The faith in ritual is strong and commonly shared.

Wairimu means *"giant."*

She was the first woman who took the courage to speak up, she told a story of how the spirit (of Earth) attacked her. She had trouble walking but it did not end with her, her children also nearly died. All medical efforts were not helpful. She narrated her painful experiences. She also explained how she got some relief after doing the necessary rituals.

Achieng means *"born when the sun shines."*

She spoke about the juju attack sent to her and the damage it caused to her family. She lost her health and wealth. She was clearly warned by the juju priest some years before that such thing was going to happen to her if she did not fulfill the oath she made. Because of circumstances, she could not fulfill the oath and she is now dealing with it.

Hibo, or **Hiba**, means *"gift."*

This woman talked about her ordeal when the spirit of the forest descended on her. She traveled to another continent for healing but the forest bath she did there did not give her the needed relief. She is still dealing with it.

Abimbola means *"born with honor."*

She spoke and continued her story of the painful experience with the spirit of the forest. "I was helpless in the violent way I was used. It was by force. I had no strength to resist. I had to learn to accept it as my lot. This was after someone taught me how to go about it."

Bontu means *"proud."*

This woman did not elaborate much but added that she and her partner were both used at the same time by the same spirit. She could see how her partner was being used, and the partner could also see how she was being used. She could not understand how one could use a male and a female at the same time.

Dayo means *"joy arrives."*

Spirit of the forest story.

"There was always tension and restlessness in my house. I would feel that there is the presence of someone. Occasionally, it felt as if someone was looking at me and that I was not alone. Sometimes, I would hear things fall as if someone was looking for something. It often happens in my kitchen. There is just restlessness and no peace and serenity in my house. I later found out that the presence was real and I had to carry out a ritual to send it out."

Eshe means *"life."*

Spirit of forest story.

She spoke about how she lost her job and then countless incidents followed in a sequence that made her know that it was not a coincidence. She went searching and got information on how somebody sent the spirit to torment her.

Imani means *"faith."*

She spoke about the health hazard caused by Hoodoo to her. She did not keep a promise she made after a ritual for many years. She had even forgotten about the promise and the incident. When she got the problems, a family member inquired and informed her of the cause. Only then did she remember it.

Ime means *"patience."*

Spirit of snake story.

"It is our family godhead and we brought offerings to it. I thought that living abroad would end the relationship and the covenant but it came to me in a dream several times and warned me. It spoke to me like a snake speaking to somebody. Initially, I was afraid, but later I got used to it. Now my health is not good enough, and I cannot afford what is demanded. I must go and do the ritual when I have the means. I have been sick for many months and there is no solution."

Nenhle means *"beautiful day."*

She spoke about a voodoo bath she took to solve her voodoo problem and how things turned out to be worse for her. It cost her a lot to take a flight to the continent and to find the shrine and perform the ritual. She does not know what she can do to get well.

Nneka means *"my mother is supreme."*

Spirit of air story.

She had a commitment to the spirit because of a covenant made long ago in the family lineage. It affects her, and she never took it very seriously until she lost most of her sight and got many more problems.

Zuri means *"beautiful."*

The disturbance of the ancestor's spirit of her family. She just got sick. Different diagnoses were done, but the cause could not be found. "I called my family to tell them about it and a few days later they called me back and said that my ancestors wanted food from me. As the firstborn, my responsibility is to give them food every year. But because of Covid-19, I could not travel that year and I forgot about it. I gave the order to provide them with what they need. It was done, and my health problems disappeared just like that."

Nnenna means *"father's mother."*

She spoke about an Umbanda torture to her. She narrated the blood sacrifices carried out to help her out, and she also narrated the attack and how it turned into a nightmare.

Rufaro means *"happiness"*

Having a child was difficult for me. I went for some help and during the visit to the shrine, I did a sacrifice. Afterward, I got pregnant as was promised to me and I had a boy. My son is not healthy mentally. Many institutions have treated my child unsuccessfully. They give him many kinds of disorders, but nothing is helping. I know the truth and I know what to do. I cannot talk to the psychiatrist or doctor about the truth. I have to go back to the shrine to make some sacrifices. But the person is no more, and the shrine is no more. There is no other place I can go to get help except for that particular spirit who helped me to be pregnant. Every day I live in pain in seeing my child crazy knowing what I did."

Thema means *"queen."*

She shared a story of a marriage with a spirit who warned her not to love her children and her husband otherwise all of them would die before her eyes. Any child she loves more will be sick and suffer psychological problems. Any child she got attached to will have the same problem. The children were kept away from her. The same thing applied to the husband. They can quarrel for nothing. Even what type of tea to drink may start an argument, even though they have many kinds of tea in the kitchen. They can be peaceful and joyful but in a split second, they can have quarrels. "One day, I had to make a choice to divorce my husband or separate from the spirit husband. In my dream, I understood that my spirit husband is from my family with the permission of my parents. My husband, I chose against the will of my parents.

Therefore, my family continued to support my spirit husband and did not support my husband. After all, I was married to my spirit husband since childhood. I was also told that divorcing my spirit husband means damage to my life and my children, also it will have negative effects on my parents. I divorced my husband. But the problem is not yet over. My new partner is also facing the same hardships which my former husband had. Sickness, accidents with the car, and a lot of strange health issues. Life is heavy."

Hiwot means *"life."*

She told the story of how many things in her house got damaged in a few days. It started with her gas cooker which she repaired, and it broke again within two days, and she had to buy another one. Then water leaked from the pipe in the wall which made her have to change the ruined floor and other things continued until she had no money to repair anything else. She realized that it was not a coincidence that all those things were happening at the same time. She had to carry out a ritual to stop the spirit that was responsible for that. This ritual was done more than ten thousand kilometers away from where she is living. She noticed that the ritual worked when the problem ceased and there was harmony in her house.

Nontle means *"beautiful girl."*

She narrated a story of her dream where she was bound by her hands and legs and laid to be killed. She has to carry out a ritual to heal from the sickness which started a day after her dream.

Lerato means *"love."*

She spoke up and said how she could not marry or stay in a relationship because of the spiritual marriage she was involved in. She narrated her attempt to end it, but the spirit partner was determined to kill her. Any relationship she enters is like torture to her and her partner. Her longings and desires are never fulfilled. Her intense demands for her partner are never enough. The spirit tortured her with not being satisfied by anybody. It does not matter what the partner gives, it is never enough. She will not belong to any partner except to the spirit. Most of her interaction with the spirit is in dreams. She is getting the right help presently, which gives her some relief.

Nnenne means *"mother's mother."*

She narrated how she was seeing the spirits of the dead family members in her house. When she is walking on the street, they follow her. She would ask some people to stay close to her but when she stands with people, they wait for her to be alone. It was giving her sleepless nights. She started thinking about suicide because the spirits were telling her to commit suicide. On the street, they would be telling her what to do. She needs a lot of strength to walk on the street and to be with people. It is like a constant torture to her. She does not have any rest. It is stressful living with it.

Noxolo means *"peace."*

She told a story of how her son killed someone just in a few split seconds. He was a very normal man, and nothing was happening to him. He just took a knife and killed his brother. Thereafter, he became normal again. The police took him. We later found out that a spirit was sent to him who took over, and after he killed the brother, the spirit left him. The brother did not do anything wrong. It was a punishment for the family because the parents did not carry out the sacrifices assigned to them. "The loss of my son was the price we paid. We had to carry out the ritual in the continent where we come from."

Mpho means *"gift."*

"My son rejected the girl who was betrothed to him when both were a baby. My son wanted to marry someone else. The girl and her mother went and did something which made my son crazy and useless. We have tried all we could, but there is no one to heal him. He is at home and his situation is getting worse every year. The girl is now married and has children. I regretted doing that when he was born. I also never thought she would do such a thing to my son."

Oluchi means *"God's work."*

"I woke up one morning and I felt like a child of five years of age. That is the image I had of myself. I dressed to go to work. When I came to the street, my foot seemed like it was sticking to the ground. My leg felt very heavy and looked like an elephant's leg. When I managed to come to the zebra crossing to go to the other side of the street, I became afraid. I saw myself as a child of five and I could not put my feet on the zebra crossing. A voice told me that I was too young to cross over, so I went back home. I called my doctor, but she wanted to see me, and I could not go to her. For many days I could not go out until some people who were missing me at work came to pick me up to come back to work. One of them took me to my house doctor.

My doctor said that she couldn't help me, and she gave me a referral letter to the hospital. They did some diagnoses including scanning but found nothing. My doctor also gave me a referral letter to the psychologist. After telling my story to the psychologist, she said she couldn't help me either. I noticed that my story was strange to her as she looked surprised and confused. She did not send me to any other person, and she did not give me any advice. It was then that fear started growing within me. I thought I would die. I have four children to care for. I cannot go to work. Then, somebody who heard my story came and carried out some rituals, and that feeling left me. I did not see myself as a child anymore. I saw myself at the correct age of 49 years. My feet were not sticking to the ground. The fear of stepping on the zebra crossing left me. The woman who carried out the ritual was 87 years of age. She told me that she has a lot of experience with this health problem. She advised me on what to do if it comes back. When I do those things, I can still go out and carry out my daily activities. This is what I was doing until I found the source of that health problem. I confronted it and it stopped.

Rudo means *"love."*

"Every week I suffer from migraines. Sometimes it is so severe that I can not think well or see very well with my eyes. I went to my house doctor for several months, who kept on giving me medicine for headaches. The medicine was not helping. After some years, I met a man who carried out a ritual that ended the headache. The source of the headache was a spirit related to my family. I have been free from it for many years now."

Abeni means *"we asked for her, and behold, we got her."*

"I wish sleeping would not be necessary for my life. When the evening comes, I am afraid to go to bed. Every night when I go to bed, I have a nightmare. I know I will be attacked by people who are trying to kill me. They are mean and have different weapons. I often escape them. It goes on the whole night. I wake up sweating and gasping. My heartbeat will be high. I will feel tired like someone who ran kilometers of a marathon. Going to bed to sleep turns into a horror for me. It makes me weak, and I cannot concentrate during the day."

Hafsat means *"gathering."*

"Back pain tortured me for many years. One strange issue is that my father had the same pain. I nearly went crazy because of the pain. I took every possible treatment from the doctors, but it did not help me. When I performed a ritual, it all went away, and I did not suffer it again."

Nomusa means *"merciful."*

She narrated her dream of seeing a child. She has a child with her husband and another child she sees in the dream. But she used to see that child in her dream even before she got married. The child started as a baby. Every night, she dreams, and this child comes and she takes care of him. She witnessed the growth of this child from when it was a baby to walking and becoming a teenager as the years went by. She realized that it was real when she saw how her son grew from a baby to a teenager. She still meets this child in her dream. She does not understand how such a thing is possible. She has accepted her lot that she cannot live with a man, especially the father of her son because of the father of the son that she sees in her dreams. No ritual has helped her out. Only a life alone is torture, and the feeling that she and a man will be punished with death if she has a relationship with one makes life difficult.

Another 17 women shared the same kind of experience. I will just mention a few of them who I will call Mi Lulit, means "pearls", Lindiwe means "waited for, AwaitedIfiok means "wisdom, knowledge", Adaeze means "King's daughter", Emen means "peace", and Farai means "rejoice."

Some of these women started the experience at the age of five years old and some were older. It is an experience where they were sexually abused in a dream. When they told their parents, the parents told them that it was normal, but they did not find it normal. They only understood more when they grew up and they were told to be friendly with the man who comes to meet them in the dream. Almost all of them ended up not having good relationships with men. Some remain single. Some of them, who happened to do the right ritual, now have a good relationship with their husband.

Hlengiwe means *"helped, rescued, redeemed."*

This woman shared the story of eating in the dream and becoming sick. She remained sick for a long time, but after a ritual, she was healed.

Some other women spoke on other issues such as the fear of water. They are afraid of seeing water. One stated that she has her blackout window curtain always closed because when she looks out of her window, she will see water and she will become afraid. This has to do with her experience while traveling across water in the night. She was often invited by spirits to come out of the boat into the water. It's difficult living in the Netherlands because there is water everywhere.

Another woman narrated that she passed through the Mediterranean Sea many years ago. She still sees herself on top of the sea, as if her spirit was left behind there. While she is awake and in her sleep, she sees the water and things that happened there.

There was a story of one woman which was confirmed by many others who passed through the same Mediterranean Sea. So many people were in the water waving to them to step out of their boats to jump into the water and come to them. Although they were warned beforehand that they would see such things, they should not leave the boat to go to them. Some of them still have the image printed in their mind. That is why they are afraid of boats or water.

The experience in the rescue boat on the Mediterranean Sea more than a decade ago made it difficult for a few of the women to use a car or any moving object. They still feel that they are going to vomit on the moving object.

All the narrated stories and the majority of others I did not share here, especially from men who did not get the right medical attention. They are left to solve it themselves.

Some psychologists, psychiatrists, specialists in health care, and family doctors I consulted admitted that they do not have a clue about what to do with the stories. They also do not know where to send them for help.

Chapter 4

CULTURE

Aïchatou means *"alive."*

It was a market day. They were many people in the market who were buying and selling as usual. There was an explosion that was not too loud. People started running away from the scene. Some people started running towards the scene. The confusion lasted for a few minutes before the information was spread. There was a man who was healthy and was shopping, but suddenly, his stomach busted open. The content of his stomach was spread around. He died instantly. There was no bomb, and there was no thunder and lightning. No one touched him.

The information happened to be that he was suspected of a crime, which he denied. The community did not believe him and took him to a shrine. He swore before the deity of the shrine that he was innocent of the accused. The community left him to the mercy of the deity.

It was believed that the deity would follow him wherever he went and would act against him if he was guilty. That became the cause of his death in the community market day for the public. The deity showed the community what its judgment is.

It is also a way to ingrain fear and horror in the life of the community members who want to hide the truth and tell lies to the community and even to the deity. The judgment of such a godhead is straight and instant. This is an example of how people experience the spirit and why they are afraid. The spirit who is sent after them is always close to them.

OATH & RITUALS

The fear of the spirit is instilled in many forms.

As I already stated, Africa does not have a written document culture, the spirit is the witness, lawyer, and judge but also the punisher of the victim. When the spirit is invoked and the victim is left in its hands, one never knows what the outcome will be. In some cases, what one witnesses is what follows as what we see happening in society. Namely, people who are afraid to discuss the spirit that they feel is the cause of their problems.

The oath goes together with rituals. Rituals make the oath stronger and more binding to the spirit. All rituals are the avenue of the covenant with the spirit, it is an important part of oath-taking. Therefore, rituals are used in promise-making. It is used in swearing. It is used in taking an oath of office or position. It is also used in declarations. It implies that the god, deity, or godhead will act if the person does not keep their word. The person will come before the deity and agree on something he will do or something he will not do. The person will pledge something which relates to him. The vow is sealed in the ritual with words and rites.

After such acts of agreement, the person can travel even outside of Earth, because it does not matter where the person travels to. The spirit will be there to act against him if he does not fulfill the agreement.

In this case, there is nothing like changing the writing paper or going to court. The gods are in charge. There will not be any possibility of bribery or fraud. Keeping the agreement is the solution and safety.

There is no book, no person as religion founder to follow, and no scientific agreed approach. That is the African way. Nobody claims ownership of certain knowledge or discovery. Nobody is the founder of the religion or God and godhead. Africans have a religion suiting their worldview. African Traditional Religion (ATR) helps Africans in difficult times like any other religion. The religion is part of African culture. It forms African spirituality. Spirituality and culture go together. Africans, therefore, do not have a scientifically agreed-upon approach to the spirit realm. There are therefore no rational analyses of what the spirit realm is like. The approach remains accessible through the senses. The senses are responsible for basic information accumulation and the learning process.

The senses play an important role in all aspects of culture in Africa. I will look into the four aspects that are basic in African culture. Some I will just mention briefly because other cultures share the same. Others I will elaborate on because it is somehow unique in African culture. The four important aspects that are in every culture are: Words, Dreams, Spirituality, and Rituals.

RESILIENT

AFRICAN WOMEN

Chapter 5

WORDS

African words contain wisdom transferred from ages of knowledge. It often goes with working power. The words are often meant to achieve results. Therefore, they are often carefully chosen. It can be a word spoken for a curse or for a blessing. Blessing and cursing are done with words. These are examples of words with negative or positive consequences. Words can hurt us or make us happy.

It can be spoken out of anger or joy. In short, manifesting takes place in language and has a purpose. The use of words is learned in your cultural context.

Language takes place within communication. Communication is sending and receiving phenomena. Both language and communication take place in a specific context. The social, cultural, and space/environmental contexts are considered important in Africa. Things you spoke to someone in private are less powerful and easily put aside than what you said to a person in public. Public utterance implies social and community witness, and they have a heavier weight than when done in private. Such utterances in social contexts can only be withdrawn and canceled in social contexts. For example, one cannot call a person a wicked man in public and in private to tell him it is a joke or a slip of the tongue. He has to go back to the same social gathering where he said such a thing and tell the hearers that it was a joke or a slip of the tongue. This is just an example, but there are many other examples like what you can say in the presence of children and the words one can or cannot use.

The same applies to the use of words to women, men, brothers, sisters, leaders, and all people. There are things you can say in someone's house when you pay them a visit, and things you cannot say. When it comes to quarrels between brothers or family members, such issues are not settled in the house of a family member. It is discussed on neutral ground either be it in an open place, under a tree, or in the family general hall. The purpose of choosing this place is because the whole family, both human and spirit, are present at such hearings. Both the humans and spirits will give their verdict. The idea of a neutral place is because the spirit may refuse to leave the house after the hearing is over. Such presence may cause restlessness for the family member. Another reason is that when you are in someone's house, you are not allowed to use harsh words to him.

It may lead to unexpected results or violence. One is supposed to feel more powerful in his house. It is not the place for one to use words to challenge the house owner. These are examples of context. In most cases the offender must go to the house of the victim to talk about the issue. In some cases, the one who seems stronger and powerful must go to the house of the weak and less privileged. The idea is to give the weak or the victim more privilege to express himself because of being at home advantage over the visitor. The basic rule here is that safety of the visitor must be guaranteed. Issues that are yet too fresh and painful should be treated in neutral ground and especially in shrine were the use of harsh words are extremely minimized. You do not use harsh words in the presence of the gods. It is a mark of lack of respect to the gods which can have destructive effect. The gods always demand respect in expression.

The use of words in social and cultural contexts includes the social relationship and the type of relationship between the communication partners. This aspect of culture is something one learns in childhood. The use of words and communication in language goes further than human communication. It goes further than communication with a spirit, the unseen world. The use of words in communication towards the spirit is also different. You can come across them further in this book. Because this is an upbringing that starts when one is a baby, it is not something one can learn at an adult age. The soul of those words and the context in using them are not easily learned.

As I wrote earlier, Africa is a culture of senses and it is not logical or rational. Intellectual and rational is not highly appreciated. Knowledge, understanding and wisdom are highly applauded. Africa is a biological culture with biological thinking. In other words, they think as human beings behave. They think as nature behaves. Human behavior is as humans are, namely biological. Removing the bio and keeping the logical is strange to Africans. This is important to understand in communicating with Africans. It is not something one can learn anywhere.

There is no institute or training that can teach someone this aspect of culture, going into the depths and feelings contained in the words and where to use them. Each language tribe or community in Africa owns this soul of communication, which is inaccessible to outsiders. Therefore, no outsider can be competent in communicating with people in that tribe or community. Being culturally competent is impossible in African culture, not only because it is an oral culture, but because it is interwoven in communication and in the use of language of the community both human and spirit which makes it impossible.

This is necessary to note. The use of sensitivity in dealing with African culture needs attention. Africans communicate with their soul, body, and spirit. In other words, Africans communicate with their whole being. This communication is expressed in senses and understood as such. Majority of the communication are without words or verbalization.

Understanding this sensitivity means that you know something about the African culture, and you know where your border is. Only a born African can speak of being competent in African culture. When the women called me and said that the health care professionals do not understand them, I easily understood why it was so. Healthcare professionals are not born Africans. Those who are born learn their profession in another culture. The barrier or gap is big.

Africans communicate the way they think. Thinking and communication go together. The mouth speaks what the heart is filled with. The organs of the body expresses what is alive in the body.

Africans think in the round. You can see that in how they build their houses. You can also see that in how they plan their lives. Having children and striving for offspring is to keep the circle intact. The belief in reincarnation is not separate from this thought. The deceased come back and are actively involved in the lives of the living. There they are also given their own physical place within the family. They are taken care of with food and drink. Conversely, they also take care of the living.

Metaphysics is not something behind reality, but something physically real. Metaphysics then does not exist as such. The invisible shows a visible presence. Like the wind is invisible, even the whirlwind, storms, and tempests show visible evidence, but you cannot see it or touch it or hold it. You can feel it. That is how Africans see the reality behind the visible and material.

If an African has pain in his hand, healing is sought for the whole body. That is an example of holistic thinking.

LANGUAGE AND WORDS

Each culture speaks and thinks differently. Such thoughts are expressed in words and language.

Africans honor idiomatic expressions and parables in speaking. The leaders do not use any kind of vocabulary they want. They must be dignified words. Words of integrity and respect. The culture implies that you cannot say bad words to someone, even if you think it. You do not say something that may have negative repercussions on you. You have to check how you present words because the spirit of that word may affect you. If you speak evil to someone who is innocent, the spirit will use the word to work against you. If they find out that the person is innocent, they will avenge that person on the speaker. You are judged in spirit by what you say about yourself, too. If a curse is laid on you, and you repeat it by telling someone, it may affect you even if you are innocent. The spirit will say that you spoke it out against yourself.

This is why it can be confusing when communicating with Africans. One has to listen carefully to what is said and how it is said. For example, if Onini says to Bella. Bella, you will die. When Bella relays the word of Onini to other people, she will say that Onini said to her that Onini will die, not Bella. Bella tries to avoid repeating with her mouth the negative curse of Onini on her. This is to avoid Bella putting that curse on herself with her mouth. This example shows the use of words and language which does not end in the communication between the two namely Onini and Bella but also putting into account that spirits are involved in the communication.

When you ask an African to save money for the future so that he will not face poverty and will be able to pay for his health bill when he is sick. You may end up facing a serious quarrel with that African. He will conclude you are negative and evil-minded, prophesying his future with poverty and sickness. He must not prepare for disaster and crisis before it is there. Preparing for it means you are calling and expecting it. In that sense, the spirit will arrange it for you, and it never fails.

Therefore, asking an African to prepare for his pension years while he is young is like cursing someone. It is thinking negative about life because one expects evil in the future and that is why he has to prepare for it. Such future thinking is not there. The future means something different. All these kinds of things are expressed in the use of language. If you do not know the thinking. Then it is difficult to understand the communication involved in it.

The use of language differs much. Though languages and tongues differ, there is a common cultural belief that words create and call things into existence. Words are stronger than things like steel, stones, iron, pebbles, wood, bricks, and many other materials fearful to destroy human life. Words matter a lot. It is a two-edged sword that can cut through the flesh and bone marrow.

Words are spiritual and not material. Spiritual gives birth to the physical. Spiritual is more powerful than physical. Any physical creation took place first in mental conception and then in words, followed by communication in the language. Words create from spiritual conception to the physical realm.

> Words are not taken lightly, especially
> when it has a disastrous aim.
>
> Words are not innocent.
>
> Words have the power to achieve something.
> It creates images and calls things into existence.
>
> Words are spiritual when spoken to physical
> people and spirits.
>
> With words, you can edify and also acquit.
>
> With words, a person can be locked in prison.

You can bind someone or liberate someone with words. Words can gather, divide or disperse people. We use words to call for gathering and disperse the gathering. We use words to unite or separate people. In marriage, the words are what binds people and also what separates them in divorce. The power of bondage is stronger in words than in iron. Words can bind for generations which iron cannot achieve. Feelings and emotions are transferable with words even kilometers away.

Words can make one happy and gives joy.

Words can make people angry and furious.

Words can lead to violence or to peace.

Words can move people or stop them.

Words carry energy in them.

The tongue and the lips are marvelous instruments for creating words and voicing them out.

Words can move legs and hands and minds to action.

Words can lock up or set free.

Words can wash away.

Words can kill or cause destruction.

Words give life or joy.

Words can cause safety or insecurity.

Words can threaten, instigate fear, and give courage or hope.

Words are used in declaring war or peace.

Words can give hope or create despair.

Watch your words and what you establish with them. Stones, irons, bricks, woods, and weapons can break my bones and bruise my flesh.

Words can break my spirit, my heart,
my resilience, and my energy.

Words are violent. That is why it is called verbal violence.

Words can carry on violence for decades and even centuries.

Words can carry love for centuries and millenniums.

Africans have an expression that goes like this; the mouth that speaks can forget, but the heart that hears seldom forgets. That shows the power of words to the hearer. Words are like poison that enters the body and slowly destroys it or they are like healing medicine that enters the body and slowly heals it.

A curse spoken by words can have an effect for many generations even for those that did not know anything about it. The power of words does not end where and when it is spoken. Physical violence can affect one person or community physically involved. Verbal violence can affect the person or community anywhere they are. This can be passed on to generations. It is the words that create such things.

Africa's culture tries to protect the tongue in the use of words to avoid causing victims of the careless tongue. This is why children are trained to be quiet and listen while the adults are speaking. They have to listen to learn how to speak and use words wisely and safely. The tongue should be used with strict policy. It has the power to cause the destruction of life. It has in it sweet and sour and also bitter sides. Though it is not a big organ, actually it's one of the smallest organs of the body, but it can destroy the whole body and tribe with its actions.

Words are open doors and walls.

Words are balsams to the heart.

Words are pebbles to the soul.

Words are violent weapons to the spiritual well-being.

Words cause warfare.

Words make peace.

Words are not innocent, especially when authority speaks it. Africans are courteous with words.

Words can set fire or quench it
African culture does not take words lightly.

It is a window to the heart and mind of the speaker.

Chapter 6

DREAMS

A STORY

Aberash means *"giving of light"* or *"shining."*

"I was walking on the street in an African country not far away from the border of the Mediterranean Sea. I was stranded on my way to Europe. I thought I would die there. I had gone through all possible tragedies and crises. Several times I nearly died. I had lost hope of continuing my journey. One afternoon, in the heat of the midday Sun, I saw countless white maggots. They were together, but there was no cadaver or dead body there. Normally, you cannot see them in midday, especially in the heat of the Sahara Desert Sun. it was rare to see them on the street. I knew it was an omen. I thought it was a message to me. When I took a nap that afternoon, which lasted about 15 minutes, I dreamed of my brother telling me that he had died in my place to make sure my journey went well to liberate the family curse. I woke up and cried. The same day, I called my family to hear that my brother died a day earlier. It was when I knew that my journey must succeed to Europe. It was the dreams I had that helped me take the right decisions and talk to the right people who helped me."

Dreaming is a topic I will not emphasize much on. It is something human beings have almost every day. The difference is the meaning one attaches to it. Africans attach much meaning to dreams. Dreams are communication from deities, godheads, God, or spirits. There are different types of dreams. All the types have the same purpose, but only often depends on the type someone can handle. Dreaming while asleep is one type. It can be a nightmare.

There is also a lucid dream that one can feel physically while it is happening. That kind of dream can be remembered for decades.

There is also a trance type of dream. One can be brought into a trance or can go into a trance. A trance is often used in communicating with the spirit. Going into a trance to contact a spirit who will take over the body and communicate to the human being is very normal. Some tribes trace the history of their tribe with trance. The spirit that enters the body of the person can speak and tell the stories of the tribe, maybe from centuries before. There is also a vision. Africans love visions because they are interested in what the spirit world is willing to do and what is planned for the human. In fact, anything concerning senses and information through senses is welcome by Africans.

Dreams, especially visions, are often seen as a medium of communication from the spirit world to those who are afraid to see the spirit physically speak. When someone is afraid to face a spirit to talk to him, such a spirit comes in a dream to speak to that person. When the person is not afraid or has shown interest in communication, the spirit does not need to dream but can come physically to talk to that person. I will illustrate this with a story someone shared.

A STORY

Patricia

"With a calabash containing water and a cup in my hand, I went to the family shrine. It is in front of our house. There is a shrub about one meter high. My grandmother told me that anytime I want to pray, I should go there and pray. She told me while praying to offer something to it. I used to see her pray there. I used to see my parents pray there. As I was praying, I took a cup of water and poured it on the shrine. I continued this until I finished my prayer request and promises. I took my calabash and cup and left. A few hours later, I saw a big python come out there and it passed through our house. My grandmother was watching it and told me not to disturb it. She told me that it is our family deity. It came to inform me that my prayer is heard. She pointed to something on the wall to me. I turned back to continue watching the Python pass us from the door. I saw it no more. It just disappeared within a fraction of a second. My grandmother said, it just physically appeared to show me that my prayer is received. In some cases, it can come in the dream and speak to you. I had sometimes dreams where snakes and pythons speak to me. In such cases, I become afraid of seeing snakes speak. But the physical appearance of my grandmother's presence was not fearful to me.

This kind of story is rampant within African communities. The spirit often chooses to appear physically in the form of an animal or in human form and show themselves and disappear again. But they can also choose to appear in a dream. Because of this, Africans see dreams as reality. In some cases, the dreams are clearly understood. In other cases, they go to a consultation with mediums to understand the message coded in the dream.

Chinwendu, means *"God owns life"*

"On the dying bed of my father, he wanted to provide information to my mother. But my mother refused and said he should not die. My father called my brothers to talk to them about the things he wanted them to know, but they were unable to listen. I was also asked by him to listen to his message, but I refused. He called one of the nurses treating him and gave her some messages for the family while we were there in the hospital. He eventually died. We noticed afterward that we were not prepared to accept his death. After his death, he appeared to different board members of organizations and institutions where he was treasurer. He narrated to them precisely where the organization's file is kept in his house. His house contains twenty-one rooms. He explained exactly where the file was kept and where the money of that particular organization was kept. He explained how much it is to the last coin. When those people started coming to our house with the concrete and detailed information of the room and the place, we were amazed. Some money was hidden in the ceiling of a particular room. We never knew that there was an opening in those ceilings. He hides it there to protect it in case the armed robbers, who know he is responsible for the money come to the house, will not find it. The people he sent explained how the money was wrapped and the exact amount. It was then we realized what he fervently wanted to tell us when he realized that he was going to die. Those people he sent never doubted anything he told them in the dream. They all concluded that he used the word "what I tell you is the truth and nothing but the truth, anyone who doubts the accountability I give is a liar".

My father appeared to many people in dreams and visions, but never to my mother for message purposes. He knew that my mother was afraid. The only time he appeared to her was when he came with my mother's father, who already died. Both came. My father touched my mother on her buttocks, where she had an injection abscess for more than a decade that no one could treat. My mother's father touched her head and removed something from her head. That night, both the abscess disappeared and the migraine my mother suffered for scores of years disappeared until today. That was the only time my father appeared to my mother since he died more than two decades ago. Most of his communication to the family was through dreams."

Africans believe strongly in dreams as a medium of communication from the spiritual realm. There is a strong belief that nothing happens in the physical realm without the spirit showing or communicating it beforehand in the spirit realm. This is done through dreams and sometimes through seers. The seer is contacted by the spirit if the person to whom the information is communicated through a dream did not listen or understand. Then the spirit goes to the seer for a final approach. The spirit takes this measure when the information is important or catastrophic to the person or community. The dream's information is often meant to prepare or correct something to prevent pain or crisis.

The well-known stories like Pharao's dream of seven thin cows who ate up the seven fat cows and remain the same in size. Looking for the meaning of that dream which Joseph interpreted to him saved many communities from famine. The dream of Joseph who has to take Jesus and run to Egypt to avoid Herod killing the newborn baby is also an example of belief in a dream. Though, this is not mainly special to Africans. Dreams have changed the world we live in.

I will just mention a few names who believed in dreams and thereby caused big changes in the world.

It was the dream Paul had that made him cross over to Macedonia and brought Christianity to Europe. The role of Christianity in the history of European civilization proved how the belief Paul had in dreams brought Christian civilization there.

The dream of the president of America, President Abraham Lincoln. As story told it, President Abraham Lincoln dreams of a corpse lying in the White House. President Lincoln asked someone standing, "Who died in the White House?" They replied that the president died of assassination. Then, the president was assassinated. In African thinking, the president could not have died of assassination if he had taken the dream seriously and done counter rituals by the spirit realm.

Africans have many forms of understanding the physical manifestations of spirits and their message outside the dream world. The manifestation through animals can take different forms depending on the message being communicated. Such spiritual message in physical forms is termed to be an omen. It can be a bad or good omen. When it is a bad omen, a quick solution is searched to stop it from happening. This solution could only be possible by the spirit.

Some omens are negative and some are positive. In each case, one has to find out what the omen tries to communicate. Like in the dream, Africans never doubt the omen. It is a personal or a

community risk to doubt omens.

Some examples are:

Seeing many bees for no reason.

Seeing countless ants for no reason.

Seeing many flies together for no tangible reason.

Seeing night animals in the afternoon for no reason.

Seeing special-colored snakes appearing for no reason.

Chidinma, meaning *"God is Good"*

"I was walking with a neighbor in the bush. We were two women. We saw a Leopard. We knew running away was useless because we were too close. It was sleeping on the trunk of the tree that fell on the ground. I had a machete with me and the other woman did too. While walking in the bush, you must have a machete in case a snake attacks you. When I saw it was sleeping, I decided to kill it or wound it so that it will not attack us and harm us badly. The other woman was afraid and did not know what to do. I knew that if we turned back and walked away, it might wake up and come after us. I silently tip-toed like a predator toward it.

I came so close. I raised my hand with my machete. With a stroke of the machete, I aimed at its neck to cut it off. Miraculously, my machete did not touch the leopard but cut deep into the wood it was lying on. Immediately, the leopard woke up, it looked at me and stood up. The other woman shouts and tells me to run. She was paralyzed with fear and could not run. She stood like a frozen person. It was when it stood up, I saw its huge protruding stomach. It was pregnant and was about to give birth. The leopard looked at me again and slowly walked away with difficulty. I felt strange feelings as if I had just encountered a spirit. It was when I noticed that it was not an animal as I thought before. It was a spirit that carried a message to me. I felt bad attacking it.

The next day I got information that my immediate younger sister who was pregnant gave birth. When I inquired when she gave birth, it happened that she was giving birth around the time I had the encounter with the strange leopard. It was when I understood why my machete did not touch the leopard. The leopard was a symbol of my sister's spirit. If had I killed it, my sister could have died in the child delivery room."

RESILIENT
AFRICAN WOMEN

Chapter 7

SPIRITUALITY

African spirituality is what makes an African behave and do what he does. His habit is formed and informed by the culture. The culture is expressed in their spirituality. Spirituality is showing the worldview of Africans. The African worldview is decisive in African care ethics. Ethics and morals are formed in the core concept of human and spiritual relationships.

Understanding this relationship creates the possibility of understanding the Africans. The conception of God and man denotes how life is perceived and lived. The African puts this in a structure I will describe under spirituality. There is a place for everything, both visible and invisible. The invisible cannot be felt but can be experienced. In the same manner that you experience wind and air without seeing them.

The invisible is a reality to reckon with during your whole life. This is not a question of belief or not. The reality is there and does not ask for your belief or doubt. The law of gravity does not ask whether you believe in it or not.

If you disobey, you face the consequences. If you jump down tens of meters high without respecting the law of gravity by taking necessary measures for your life, then you face the consequences. This is applicable to the African sense of God, Deities, ancestors, and human beings including other visible creations that are interwoven in the same reality. The whole reality of existence is perceived to be one and united. Care ethics is directed from the perception that the well-being of all is interconnected.

Africans are giving all they need to know and understand the cosmos and to be able to live in harmony by keeping the balance and respect for all creation.

The cardinal point of African spirituality is unreserved and wholehearted love to God with body, soul, and mind. God the creator has made human beings and endowed them with the whole physical and spirit attribute for creation. Keeping the spirit, soul, and body wholly sanctified for God's sake is the mission and aim of rituals. These three-in-one, namely the trinity of the body, soul, and spirit, are components of human beings given by God to share creation with Him.

The other spirit communities like deities, ancestors, elevated human beings, and physical creatures are given by God to serve in the creation and communities as established by God. God works with and through them. God needs human beings to work for human beings. That is why there are elevated human beings from the community whom God works with. Living in harmony with all of them is the first responsibility of human beings. Africans look into the three parts of the human being, body, soul, and spirit, as one and whole. Therefore, if an African has pain in his finger, the cause can be sought in the whole body. If it is not found in the whole body, it will be sought in the whole family. If the cause is not yet found, it will be sought in the whole community, both physically and spiritually. When it comes to looking for the cause in the spirit, the answer must come. With the answer comes the solution. This is important to know in African care ethics and spirituality. We will dissect the three in one parts that constitute human beings.

BODY

Africans see the body as the house we are living in. We are in the physical world and, at the same time, in the spiritual one. We need it to do business with each other on Earth. It is a house for the visible and invisible. It is where the world meets human beings.

Without the body we cannot easily touch, see, and speak to each other. We need it to relate and work together.

It is the part of human beings that perishes and becomes humus after death; though people who died appear in dreams or physically and suddenly to human beings. The body is the house of the spirit. The spirit needs to be seen and needs to communicate with human beings. Africans also believe that the body can temporarily be transited to another body. Like someone becoming a snake, another kind of animal, or a human being. They are different parts of the body.

BONES / SKELETON

The skeleton is a bone structure consisting of many parts.

Our body is made under a structure that is carefully set up to carry out activities and responsibilities for other creations.

It supports the important organs in the body.

It also protects vulnerable organs.

Africans try to make sure their bones are strong during upbringing.

A child must be trained to have strong bones, arteries, flesh, and muscles to withstand life's challenges. Those things are highly needed in the material world.

FLESH

Flesh consists of all the human tissues of the body, including muscles, skin, hair, veins and so on. Every other part that is not liquid and bones. The flesh must be strong and fit. Having more flesh is desirable, as well as being thin. More flesh shows that one can survive difficult times. It shows that one has the stamina to handle hard times. Women who are too thin are expected to have difficulty in childbearing. Having more flesh does not mean being fat.

BLOOD

The living factor of the body that transports food and consumption. It also transports oxygen. It acts as protection for the body and cleanses things that are dangerous to it. The blood contains life. Africans do not eat raw blood because it means eating life with it. But boiled blood does not have life in it. Meat with fresh blood in it is not allowed to be eaten. Africans cook meat for a long time. Drinking blood is a ritual of the covenant which is done under the guidance of a medicine man or woman. When one drinks or eats fresh blood, he has gone into covenant with the source of the blood or the oath is taken. Blood covenant is an everlasting covenant. It is not something one can break. Its effect continues until death. Anything connected with blood means a strong connection. Blood in African conception is regarded as that which sustains life by nourishing it. Spilling of the blood means depriving the body of its nourishment, defiling the ground, and, as a result, defiling the godhead in charge of the earth. When blood is shed unlawfully, it is a defilement. However, it is a sacrament and purification when spilled for a righteous cause.

Blood transmits the physical and moral aspects of the parents' bloodline to the children and sustains the family lineage. When a child resembles the father in moral and physical traits, the father can proudly say, "he is my blood". Therefore, blood explains the elements of heredity as it carries hereditary traits. It is a very important element in the African concept of family, community, and relationship. This relationship consists of physical members and ancestors. It is the blood that binds kinsmen together and defines their common descent. The notion of community is defined by blood which interweaves all members of that community, irrespective of their geographical location. In other words, a community in the African concept is a people of one blood.

BODY SOURCE OF LIVING

Africans see the body as the material part of life made up of earthly components that should be maintained with earthly materials. The body should be fed with what is made up. The food of the body are the things the earth produces. Things like carbohydrates, proteins, and minerals. Concretely talking about tubers, vegetables, and fruits. The body contains water and should also be maintained with drinking liquids.

When these things are taken in, the body does not ask the person what the person takes in or what it shall do with it. Whatever someone takes in, the body recognizes it and knows what to do with it. It will go into action immediately and work on it and use it for the well-being of the body. The body has the record of the whole family generation in it. All are stored in small components. The faces of the family for many generations are there to be seen in the living. The deceased body still appears on the face of the living. The body keeps the scores of the family's experiences. It keeps the knowledge of food consumed. The body's knowledge never fails. It is accurate and does not need to ask anyone anything. It fully knows itself.

When a person fails to maintain the body with these products, the body will shrink and die. When the body expires because of the lack of basic needs, including rest, it is given back to the ground where it comes from and provided the source of maintenance. It is assumed that what the body contains and what builds it up is earth in nature. The humus has to go back to humus and the spirit to the spirit. The ground will accept the body and consume it. Just like the body accepts what comes from the ground, consumes and uses it. The ground will use the body to produce other vegetation which will feed other living things as well. This is the circle of the body. It goes back to where it came from.

Burning the body with fire is seen as violence and therefore not accepted as the normal process of disintegrating the body.

LIFE

Life regulates and activates all actions in the body to sustain it. Life is a continuous process that has no end. It goes from the physical realm to the spirit realm. It transits from one sphere to another. This is true human existence in which, without its presence, the body dies. Life means that the person or the living thing functions as it is supposed to function. It is carrying out its functions the way it was meant to be. When somebody is still breathing or alive but is not functioning the way he is supposed to function, it means that the person is not really alive. Life has two meanings. Mainly functioning as you are supposed and expected to function. When one is not functioning as he is supposed to or expected to function, it is said that he is not alive. Only it cannot be said that he is dead. When an African says that someone is not alive, he does not instantly mean that the person is dead. He may mean that he is useless for the purpose he is made to fulfill.

SOUL

The soul is the true person. Africans believe that the soul is situated somewhere in the heart. As its name indicates, it is the seed of the heart. The soul of the heart. The heart plays a very important role in human life. The soul is the core of the heart. The soul has a direct link with the spirit. It works with the spirit. It is the spirit that leaves when the heart stops working. It is therefore connected to the heart. It is having a materialistic connection with the body through the heart. Unlike the spirit which is freer. The soul is connected to the flesh. Its material connection makes it possible to work with the senses. The most inner battle of conscience relating to the moral judgment of good and bad takes place in the soul. A battle between your spirit and your flesh. A battle between the desire of spirit and the desire of the body, the social and the material world. It, therefore, consists of the following parts: feelings, will, and mind.

FEELINGS

Feelings comprise of all emotions, longings, and desires of the body, for example: Happiness, joy, blissfulness, rejection, pain, and sorrow.

WILL

The power of freedom of choice. Choosing from different possibilities that exist. The power to make your own decision and take your action. Your conscience and morals.

MIND / BRAIN

The power to think, to have intelligence, memory, and to remember. The brain/mind is our thinking faculty. Our thinking affects our feelings. The feelings are created by emotions that are evoked by thinking. The things you see and the associations you make out of them are things that happen automatically. You can think of many things at the same time. The mind is a complicated and extraordinary part of our body. It influences your mood and feelings.

A Godly mind, or as you may call it a protecting mind, works to keep you healthy and to protect you from issues that make you sick. It must achieve this by being in a healthy state, working continuously in a miraculous way in the background to protect your mood and keep you clear-sighted.

A healthy mind is very excellent at editing and giving favorable information to your body.

THE SOUL SOURCES

This will receive more explanation because of its place in African spirituality. I will share a story that I heard when I was a child. A part of the family tradition of storytelling. Stories with in-depth meaning that opens the view of life and the cosmos in the African context.

SOUL JOURNEY

Before and after the conception ritual the moon was at its fullness. It was so bright you could pick a broken grain of rice from the porous sands on the ground. In the middle of the compound, all family members were sitting down. They were about 200 hundred. This was another family night. The eldest stood up to address the family. His name is Gabriel Egbufor. Note his first name, Gabriel, which means that he has been converted to Christianity. The criteria to become a Christian is that one has to take a European name and not his tribal name. A European name means that one is no longer under the bond of African culture but of European Christian culture. As someone elevated and rhetorically gifted, people can listen to him. He is an elevated leader both within and outside the community.

HIS SPEECH

He said, "I want to tell you a story of your life before you came into this family. Each person's story is unique, but there is something you have in common. I also have it in common with you". He continued, "We were in another world. We came from the presence of God where we lived before coming to this family. In the presence of God, there are billions of souls living there in one community under one leadership. All are alike and behave the same according to the norms and values established. Only each one has the freedom to think and free will of choice. The souls live together as one community. They are united and share everything in common. They do not have any problems or life challenges.

They are a happy community. God, who is the king of the community, is happy. There is peace and harmony. They lacked nothing. Every time, God looked at the world. He became sorrowful. The people in the world are not living a pain-free life in harmony with each other and their environment". He told them how the people in the world are living. The pains and sorrow the people are going through always pinch him. The suffering of people makes him suffer too. God senses people.

Every day, God makes an open request to all during a gathering. He will ask them who wants to go to the world to teach people how to live life like it is being done in the heavenly community. Every time God asks this question, ten thousand souls will respond and will be willing to go. He takes them to educate them about the earth and the world. Then God explains to them what the journey means and what is involved. The earth is a place where things are physical. I will explain these meanings because it is important in order for you to understand life on earth.

EARTH

The earth is dry land. There are masses of water called seas and oceans. There is also an open place called the air. This open place is the space that demarcates heaven and earth. The earth is a mass of material bodies, some hard and some soft, that produce vegetation from seed-bearing plants and fruit trees bearing fruit with seeds inside, each corresponding to its species as it was designed to be so. 'There is also every kind of living creature and species like cattle, creeping things, tame and wild animals of all kinds. It never changes.

SEAS

There are swarms of different living creatures which no one can count in the seas and oceans. Some creatures are great sea monsters and some are small. All the creatures belong to their species and multiply also in their species.

AIR

The air is where the birds fly their way above the earth across the vault of heaven. The birds multiply on land in their species. The space called the vault of air makes physical contact between the earth and heaven difficult. The heavenly and earthly bodies cannot meet without going through a transformation or having a mediator. The transformation is a very painful process. The journey from heaven to earth is not an easy one. Because of the realm one has to cross and the accumulations and programming one has to go through, the more you are loaded to be able to be effective, the greater you accumulate pains and loads.

HUMAN BEINGS

All the creations on earth are being cared for by human beings. Human beings are like us. They have our image and our likeness. They care for the fish of the sea, the birds in the air, the cattle, all wild animals, and all creatures that creep along the ground. Human beings are male, and female, and made to be fruitful and multiply among their species on earth. They are part of creation, meaning that those other creations have certain things with them in common. Their work is to care for those earthly creations. As a reward, they can have them as their food. They are dependent on the foliage of the plants as their food. The seed-bearing plants are everywhere on the surface of the earth, and all the trees with seed-bearing fruit are their food.

All the tame and wild animals, all the birds that fly in the air, and all the living creatures that creep along the ground are their food. Human beings need earthly produce to maintain their body that is made of earthly material. They need to consume earthly produce to keep their body alive and healthy. If they refuse to follow the law, their body will start to expire and return to earth. The soul will then leave when the body expires. The spiritual side of them that made them in our likeness and image is maintained in our relationship with us. This spiritual aspect is not visible. It mainly exists in the senses. They have the senses to know this and maintain it. When they lack the earthly produce to maintain their body, then they suffer physical pain. When they lack the maintenance of spiritual life in them, they suffer emotional pains. Therefore, human beings suffer much from both sides.

DARKNESS & LIGHT

Human beings live in two divisions of day and night. The day is when there is light. The light comes from heaven to shine on the earth. When it appears, the earth can see and carry out its activities. The eyes of human beings see well when there is light. The period of light is called the day.

When the light is taken from the earth, then darkness will appear. In the darkness, human beings cannot see well. They are not created to see in the dark with their eyes. Darkness is called night. But at night, we have light from heaven for them. It gives them light, but different from the light of the day. It is a smaller and softer light than the light of the day. These two lights divide darkness from light. All creation is subjected into a cycle of time. It is in the form of seasons. The lights make it possible for human beings to understand the seasons, years and to be able to celebrate festivals.

THE WORLD

The world is also something you need to understand. This is because the suffering of human beings has to do with the world. The world is a governing system that human beings set up to take care of creation. At the same time, they cultivate a culture that is working against their well-being. The governing culture of the world is where all the problems lie. This is where there is a big difference between our life here and their life there. We need to educate them on how to govern themselves to be free from the pains, both body and emotions.

At least to reduce the pains of the body and emotions. You may not understand what I am teaching you about the world until you arrive there. Though it is important to know because you need to remember what you learned to understand where you are, and what you have to do.

TRANSFIGURATION OF
THE SOUL TO HUMAN BEINGS

After a general education, each soul receives personal instructions based on its mission to the people of earth. He will prepare each of them, telling them what they must go through and what their assignment is. Each soul has a special assignment based on the needs of people on earth. This need has to do with the place that the soul is being sent to. Based on this work, the soul will choose the experience he has to go through. He will choose the family where he wants to be born. He will choose the parents who will guide him to that work and mission. After the education, God will choose one of the ten out of a thousand volunteers. Each person on earth represents ten of the thousand who could not come. Each person is chosen out of those who were not chosen.

All human beings are chosen to come to earth for a purpose only they can fulfill. When a person fails to fulfill his or her mission, the people suffer more and longer. The family that receives the soul to start his or her work on earth has a responsibility of educating that soul. The family will be informed before conception, and the child will speak to the family before going through the process of birth. The family must prepare themselves to receive this soul before it comes into the world. The family has months to be able to do this. The soul also has this period to prepare for earthly life. Going through the birthing process presents such a stressful and traumatic journey that makes the soul forget why it came and what the mission is all about.

All the strange things that have no comparison with the culture where the souls come from give lasting stress with all kinds of negative effects. The culture of the world is another barrier to the soul. We have solutions for all the barriers.

THE JOURNEYS START AFTER ONE IS CHOSEN

This is the process the soul must go through in order to arrive on earth and become part of humanity. Being part of humanity is the only way to fulfill the mission. Human beings can only accept what is theirs. Otherwise, we could have done this work from heaven.

The soul will be sent into a deep sleep. This will reduce the pain the soul goes through as it transforms into a human being. From sleep, it will be sent into a woman in the form of a seed to the family of its choice. This process remains a top secret for the soul. It is part of reproduction and the multiplying of each species. It will enter the dark womb of the woman. Inside it, the soul will be knitted and formed with body and spirit. This is done in secret in the depth of the earth. At this stage, the process is called an embryo. The soul cannot be hindered by darkness or light. It can always see even in the darkest darkness or in a highly dimmed light.

The creation of body and spirit must be a perfect work and, as a result, it takes time. This is the main period of transformation into human beings. Human life starts taking place. The soul will go through a process of forgetting who they are. It will start a process of adaptation, assimilation and integration but it still maintains its core. Those processes are painful because you will take in what is foreign to you and make it a part of you. You will become bicultural. Your origin is changed to be the place of your birth.

This process takes toils that leads you to naturalization in your new world. You will forfeit your language and speak human language. You will lack the language to describe things that human beings have no language for. You cannot explain all you want and all you know. Even your heavenly life will be a memory in your subconscious. All the life you had in heaven will sink into your subconscious. It will seem like a dream or something unrealistic to the life you will be having as a human being.

Think about the love and harmony you experience in our community here. You will long to belong to a community like this. But it will not be found. You will try to set up such a community because you will be missing it. It will turn out to be tedious work. This happens because your effort and result will be compromised and corrupted by the culture of the world. The beauty and peace you experience here in heaven is non-existent. You will sense the opposite of it. You would long to let people feel and see it so that you can make it possible with them, but there is no language to communicate it. You may speak the same words but understand different things by them. The barrier between human and soul is so great that the soul prefers to store memories in the heart. Memories can be beautiful, lovely blissfulness and some other joyful things. But there can also be painful memories like the loss of someone through death and health crisis, or even something that has to do with hatred or injustice committed against you.

Reconnecting to the former life of your soul will happen in two ways, namely through your senses or your spirit. You can hardly differentiate both. One thing is assured, you will not be left without guidance. Living human life will subject you to numerous painful experiences. When you try to maintain your soul mission, you will face many obstacles. They may declare you mad and give you all sorts of names. This is because you are doing things differently than their corrupted culture. A culture built in lies and falsehood. Therefore, they suffer.

This suffering affects you. You are a part of the community with them. At the same time, the suffering connects you more to the truth you know. The more you are connected to the truth, the more you stand alone. The truth about truth is that you stand alone. The more you stand, the more fears grow in you.

You may face hatred by some who are ready to harm you just because you are not like them. Some may try to harm you out of jealousy because you are who they want to be but could not achieve it. Their jealousy may come to such hatred that they'd like you to suffer for not being like them. Maybe your morality and character is what they desire but could not get it. Maybe you see things differently than them. The issue of loneliness may come because you have no support. Some may claim to be with you and that they understand you. Their mission may be to convert you into their own way so that you cannot fulfill your mission. This is often done by those who lost their mission and are not ready to go for it. They are afraid of losing and missing what they have. They are afraid of loneliness and missing their present desire. At the same time, they know that they are not fulfilled with what they think they have and what they do not want to miss. They are permanently in pain with the desire of their soul. They do not know which way to follow.

Your soul will be registered in the identity of the world. This is the beginning of confusion. You will start struggling with identity. The identity the world will give you is different from your identity. This is because your soul is highly protected. The memories are kept intact. Your formation in the womb and further nurturing with food, drinks, and the culture you are wrapped in are recorded in your body and memories. Your body needs that information to process automatically what you take in. When you eat or drink or take in anything, your body does not need to ask you what it is and what to do with it. It knows how to process, use it or reject it. Your soul is also doing the same with the information it has received from us.

While you will understand, every so often you can be overwhelmed. You may not understand in certain conditions. The conflicts will start in you. This is one of the worst struggles you will face in your inner self. It may lead you to doubt yourself. At a certain stage, it will lead you to start defending yourself in order to show you are not what they say. You will be searching for evidence to validate your message and your mission. This will take a toll on you. Because those whom you expect to understand you will use it against you. They will be the worst source of your social pain. Their ill talks about you will occupy your mind and weaken your inspiration. You will be subject to loneliness which you did not choose but were forced into. Such loneliness is sorrowful. One assurance is that you will not be alone, even though you may feel as such. You must realize that such experience is the cause of tragedy in human situations. In such loneliness, people withdraw and avoid contact. In that case, social change becomes impossible. The solution to their problem is undoubtedly social change. To have a community life, as we have, should be the first goal of your mission. When you come to such a situation, remember it is a process of learning about the human situation and a stepping stone for you to know what to do.

When you finally come out of it and get to your work, you will not have time anymore to listen to their ill talks about you. You will not have time because you are doing your work. You know where you are going and what work still needs to be done. You will not long or desire to have the validation of such people. You think that their validation is ultimate for you. Your work will speak for itself and for your mission. Those voices will sink into your inactive memory. Although you may use some to be an energy to keep you going instead of keeping you down. Such voices may strengthen you instead of weaken you.

One thing you can be sure is that your soul identity is intact in you. It is perfectly coded in your DNA. Your immune system runs to give you basic protection from many other dangers. With it, you truly shall never get lost. It is intact. You may not get access to it, but when it is highly needed to strengthen or support you, you will get the support. There is a system of communication between you and us. Only you can receive the information. If you do not listen, someone will be sent to inform you or remind you. Like your soul, your mission is intact, and only you know it. You may often forget it because of the pressure and difficulties in the world as well as the earthly challenges. Nothing will happen to it. Anytime you want to carry it on, you will have it present in you. It is protected from people who may want to damage it. The governing body that loves the suffering of people on earth will throw all kinds of suffering to you. Everything about you and your mission is stored in the ultimate secret of your identity and in your DNA.

When the sting of your pain becomes too much to bear, you will receive a short flash of peace, joy, and the beauty of reality. This is to strengthen you for the work you still must fulfill. It is an assurance that you are not alone. A confirmation that those who send you are witnessing and will support you. Such confirmation is like a balsam for the aching heart. It helps you not to forget that eyes are watching you to fulfill your mission because a lot of life relies on your saving mission. If you fail, they will perish.

THE TRANSFIGURATION OF BODY TO SOUL

This short flash will come like a memory to you. It will flash off many accumulated pains and suffering stored in the body. The fears accumulated by standing for the truth. Especially when doubts are creeping in, and despair is trying to subdue the soul in believing lies, and falsehood, to submit to fear and to give up its mission. This strong message shows you a glimpse of where you come from and what you are called to do. In some situations, it is done in secret with you alone. You may experience it as a trance or dream or vision. It is a means to be shown to your soul. But in some cases, depending on the condition, it may be done in the presence of others or even before the public. Some may call it wonder or miracle. Those present witnesses may come to confirm that there is power above human beings.

They will talk of transcendental power or heavenly power. Such may be done to affirm to you that your mission is relevant and to remind you where you come from. People may be flabbergasted, but to you, it remains something you remember as normal. Those present, because of what they witness, may come and support your mission.

The inspiring flash and glimpse may last for a while. You may face the storms of life afterward and forget inspiration. This can come through difficulties of life or doubt whether that glimpse was truly a confirmation. Other issues of life and world affairs may cloud your mind for a while. It may also last for a long time. The effect is that you may forget the mission you are called for. You are still not alone. People's pain runs very deep and the world is greatly in durable birth pangs. You will go through such disorders and distresses. It is necessary to achieve life's great transformations for people. As you know, regarding social life, we live and go through what is necessary. The people of earth need social change. That is the basic answer to their pain and sorrow. When you interact with them, you are affected. You cannot escape their suffering. Inside their suffering, you can start transforming social life.

As you interact with them, those who are on the same mission as you will be connected to you. They will be drawn to work together with you. The more you are connected, the more you educate others and support one another. Your example of the community you set up and share is what the world will see and follow. Through your experience, you will guide others and educate them.

The more you work with the community, the more your senses present to you who you really are. Your soul identity becomes clearer to you. Slowly, you regain awareness of where you come from. You're distancing yourself from the world. This will continue provided you do not care what the world will do to you. Fear of any kind will leave you. You will not long for anything of the world. You will not fear loneliness anymore. Hatred or rejection will be something in your dormant memory and no longer of your active memory.

LOSS

You can face the loss of important things in your life. You may lose all basic things you have gathered in life. You may even lose the things the world assumes are basic for a successful life. You may lose what seemed to be your basic identity and the things you desire so much. Such loss will bring deep suffering to you. You may think that it is the end of who you are. You may lose faith in yourself. Such moments are necessary for you to be reborn into your gift. When all those attachments and references which you accumulated in the world culture become detached from you, you may ask yourself who you are without all those things. That is the process of transitioning your soul from dependence to the independence of the world culture you identify yourself with. When all those identities are gone, you will receive a new and true one. In that true one, your talent and what is given to you to carry out will manifest. You will start experiencing the hidden identity, including gifts in you. You will learn to produce from yourself. You will tap into your inner strength and gift to work in the world. That inner strength and gift is what you need for the mission. It is what makes you unique. It is what is encoded in you for the earth. You can learn to grow from it. You will use your language and your vocabulary. You will stand for yourself and seek an institution to protect you. You will speak the truth you know and what you have seen and believed in. You will get support from us. We will be with you anywhere in the world.

You will pass through the world culture and know it without it being a part of you. You have to know it because you have to educate the world. They know. You have to speak through what they can relate to. Then you can speak to what the majority cannot connect to. However, only a few who are willing can connect. What they call suffering, you may see it as a pathway to joy. What they call good, you may see it as evil. You may not use their method of thinking. Only those who can connect will be educated. You will educate them. When you educate others, then the soul journey will continue to inspire others until many people have joined it.

At the end of the instruction, God asked the volunteers again who still wanted to go to the world to educate them on how to live together like us in a community? One is chosen out of the Ten that represents a thousand. Each person in the world is chosen out of ten from which a thousand are not chosen. Each person has the privilege to be in the world for the mission of making the world a home and community for human beings. Our ultimate call is community life. It is the cardinal point and goal of our life. A community where human beings learn how to live a life of being humans.

SOUL CARE

The cycle of life in African spirituality is a solution for the soul. It protects the soul from loneliness and suffering. Africans believe that the soul needs to be taken care of to protect it from suffering.

The most suffering you face as a human being comes from who you are. The soul suffers most because it misses where it originally comes from.It is a mystery. When something is not present, you will start missing it. You know something or someone is not there. It is remembering and not forgetting that makes you suffer from the lack of that thing. Missing is the other side of longing and desiring something that is not there. Something you remember that used to be there, but is no more. In some cases, it is gone, like in the case of death. You will not see, hear, feel, or touch, and so on. It is permanently gone. You desire it because you miss it, and you miss it because you desire it. If you miss something, you are incomplete. If you are incomplete, you remain unfinished. If you are unfinished, you are imperfect. In such a situation, your desire brings suffering. What you miss or desire remains a continuous process of the soul. It is the perfect source of lasting suffering. It is a permanent source of restlessness.

All that the soul accumulated becomes a memory of longing and desire when it is transformed. When the soul leaves the human body after death, it suffers longing for all it accumulated. Often it would rather not leave. The things the soul longs for and desires are often not present, and occasionally, they cannot be present. They are sometimes things from another entity that cannot be touched or reached. When the soul comes from its nonphysical nature and becomes part of physical reality, it longs for its nonphysical nature; a desire prevented by physical reality. The opposite is the case. Occasionally, the soul does not know what it longs for or desires. It cannot communicate it in words or any language. It cannot access it or touch it. The desire becomes stronger because in its subconscious it is certain that such a thing is there. The stronger the pain, the stronger it shows what it means to be absent.

Such things can sometimes be touched by music. The soul will feel the tunes and sounds and feel it. It can be touched by someone's voice. It can direct to the soul, and it will feel it. It can be touched by words or language. Maybe the way someone looks at you may evoke the feeling, and you will remember it. All this happens in the sense level. The moment you try to rationalize it and put it into language to explain it to others, it often gets lost or makes no sense anymore. When you know your soul, you know yourself. Knowing yourself is the ultimate knowledge of your source. Your soul shows you your place and position in creation. It is your primary goal in life to know yourself. Without it, you know absolutely nothing. You can only know from what is known. When you know yourself, you can know other things.

RESILIENT
AFRICAN WOMEN

Chapter 8

SPIRIT

The spirits are two types, namely the human spirit and the Godly Spirit. The human spirit comes from God the creator. This spirit connects us with all creation and with each other. The spirit is given to a human being by God in order to give him life in his body. Human beings are called to community life together. The spirit of God in every human being shows the same origin. Like all, human beings are made to sustain life through what comes from the ground. The spirit can only be well maintained through what comes from God. Therefore, we are from the same source and we go back to the same source. The Holy Spirit comes from God to those who ask for it. It is a special spirit for special work for creation. It is given to those who keep themselves holy. It helps them to maintain the holiness in which we are called to live.

The human spirit comprises the following parts: Intuition, conscience, godliness, and chi.

INTUITION

The power to know something in your inner self. You feel something directly, and you know it for sure without using your brain or rationalilty. You know it for sure outside your intellect. It is one of the senses. God exposes exactly how it is in your thought. God reveals it to you, and you are sure no one tells you. It is purely receiving direct and sanctified information from God. It is a truth that is not corrupted with lies or falsehood. It implies that the receiver must be immaculate before God. God does not work with a soul that is not immaculate before him. Such a soul or person should keep himself clean and have no stain in his hand and mind. Such people are assumed to be full of light and insight. They could receive and understand God's communication with them. Their intuition is developed and protected by God so that the line of communication does not have any form of intrusion from the wicked. Intuition is receiving from God without interruption or failure from the receiver. To be able to understand God, one needs wisdom. The spirit of God communicates without interception to the person's spirit. Africans have reverence for people whose intuition is highly developed at such a level.

When God speaks, the human spirit receives it. The human spirit is like a radio antenna that receives from God. A well-developed intuition is like a well-tuned receiver from God. Every human person in any culture prays and speaks to spirits, deities, godhead, God, and the invisible. Prayer is talking to invisible entities. That is why prayer is offered. When the entities reply or talk back, it is called intuition. It takes more than a listening ear to hear them speak. That is why Africans have reverence to highly intuitively developed people.

CONSCIENCE

The power to choose what is right and leave what is wrong. When you neglect your conscience, it means you heard it and rejected it. When you do this often, your conscience will be dormant and weak. When you steal for the first time, your conscience will warn you that it is not right. You will get physical signals like sweating, fast heartbeat, stress, tension, and so on. When you do it for the second time, these physical signs will be less. When you do it another time, these signs may not show again. Those who kill people always say that the first killing was the most difficult one. The rest is easy. This is because their conscience is neutralized or dead. It does not warn them anymore. The conscience becomes incapable of functioning ethically.

GODLINESS

The power to commune with God in Spirit, to honor, adore, worship, and praise Him. Worshiping God in Spirit implies that we are not using our intellect and rationality to honor and praise Him. Our spirit is not enough to do this. Our mind often overrules our spirit. That is why we need the Holy Spirit to contact God directly without the hindrance of our feelings and human understanding or mind / intellect. Unlike the body, the spirit can only be maintained by the spirit. The spirit feeds the spirit and keeps it healthy.

CHI

This part of human beings is spiritual but different from spirit, soul, life, and so on. Africans believe that each person has a personal god ascribed to him to guide him to his destiny. It means that each individual has a destiny to fulfill and that is his purpose of being born in a particular time and space. When we use the expression that someone is lucky or has good luck, we are talking about this god in the person. I could not find any word in English for this name other than god. One can say it is the image of God in human beings. When someone is unfortunate, this god in him is blamed for that. When someone is fortunate, it is ascribed to this god. When sacrifices are made for the well-being of an individual, it is directed to support the chi in guiding the person. When sacrifices are made for ill intent towards an individual, it is also directed to the chi to affect the person. When someone wants to be free from evil wickedness, then it is the chi that is set free from evil attack. Making it simpler, we can say that nobody can live without his chi. It is through chi that we greet each other. It is through chi that we respect each other.

Chi means "God, spiritual being." It is another word to express intuition or God communicating with god in human beings. It also means God in human beings and human beings in God. It means the image of God. The interwoven relationship between humans and God and vice versa. I will use a description of the village to explain how the senses are naturally developed during upbringing. It will also explain why Africans collect information without words. One may find Africans sensitive. It has to do with the environment and upbringing. I will describe a village in the Igbo tribe in West Africa. I look at Africa through tribal locations and not in colonial land maps. Talking about Africans in colonial land maps will complicate the topic because such colonial cultures are mixed with African culture. It is not my purpose to treat both cultures in an African context. Let's take a short glimpse of a village in the Igbo tribe.

UMUNUMO

I will describe the geographical setting and the environment. This will make the story understandable. When you can picture the environment, it is easier to understand how upbringing is associated with community life. Umunumo is a village in the Igbo tribe. The Igbo tribe is an area in the Sub Sahara Africa continent. The location is rich in crude oil and gas. The world consumes from it. It is not far away from the Atlantic Ocean. It is a delta area. It has a rainforest. The soil is rich in brown and orange colors. The tropical climate including the soil and rain makes the area vegetative. The plants do well there. The trees grow high and large. We have Iroko trees, Alstonia trees, Akpaka trees, mahogany trees, and many other big trees. Sporadically, we say shrubs can grow to massive trees in the area. Bamboo trees, palm trees, and palm wine trees are the most redundant trees. The big trees in the area are so close together that they form forests. The forest in the area makes it a very dark area even on a sunny day. You cannot enter it without a light on a sunny afternoon.

Some big trees are seen as holy trees which should not be cut down. It is believed that they are a living home for forest spirits. Some big trees in the community serve as a community shrine or community gathering. It is believed that in such gatherings, humans and spirits attend them because it is a general place for both. Therefore, such trees serve both human beings and spirits. It is a holy ground and a holy tree. Shrines are often situated under a big tree or trees. One has a sense of nature, with all creations living together and respecting each other. Trees are not worshiped, but the presence in the Trees and the environment are highly respected and honored. Tree plays the role of connecting the earth and the air, but also human beings and spirits. Trees are not only materials. When a holy tree should be cut down, a special ritual is done. Cutting a holy Tree down can only be done in consultation of the community and spiritual leaders. The owner cannot cut it without such consultation. Cutting it down is done on the sole purpose of safety for the community and not for its material advantage. In cases where the community are not in danger, the Tree has to fall on itself.

The rivers are full of palm wine trees that make it difficult to swim or to use nets to fish in them. The mangrove trees grow in the river. The fish like living under the mangrove trees. The rivers in my village are sources of different kinds of food. Fish are well-known, but we have numerous other foods from palm wine trees, which also give drink. The palm wine drink is used as baby food. Especially freshly tapped palm wine is given to babies as extra supplements for breastfeeding. Some women who cannot produce enough milk for their baby use freshly tapped palm wine. We do not have powdered milk. Dairy milk is non-existent in the area. Because of tsetse flies and other insects that kill cows, it is not possible for cows to exist in the area. The goats and other dairy animals are used for meat and not for milk.

Farming is the main source of income for the village. Cash crop farming is the most popular.

The forest is a home for animals like tigers, foxes, pythons, different kinds of deadly snakes, monkeys, birds, rabbits, and many other wild animals both small and big. When an elephant is located in my village, all the men gather. The professional hunters in the village will gather their guns, both long and short. Other non-hunters will take their sharpened machete and iron spear. They will go and hunt the elephant. The women and children stay indoors until the elephant is hunted down. This often takes place in the riverine area. It is the only area such big animals can parade for some days without someone noticing it. Animals like tigers, leopards, and snakes can easily enter accommodated areas in the village before someone notices them. When they are noticed, people are alarmed and they enter their houses and close the doors until the hunters surround the area and hunt them down.

Palm wine tappers are often the first to see the big and dangerous animals. This is because they are often in the bush three times a day to tap their wine. They have to tap it in the morning between 5.00 am and 7.00 am. In the afternoon between 12.00 pm and 1.00 pm. In the evening between 5.00 pm and 7.00 pm. The afternoon tapping is mainly cleaning work in the tree unless the tapping jar is filled with wine and runs the danger of overflowing before evening tapping. In that case, they will empty the jar and put in a new one. The morning and evening tapping are usually to collect the wine in the jar. The wine is fresh and they will go to the market to sell it. Because their work is mainly in odd hours when people are often at home, they tend to see things that move around.

Some animals go around when there is no noise from people. Some crime takes place when the criminals assume that nobody can see them or have less chance of seeing them. In such lonely moments, people with ill intent and criminals aim to go on their hidden businesses. The palm wine tapper is known to walk like a hunter or predator. He walks without making noise. He opens all his senses, namely hearing, seeing, feeling, smelling, thinking, intuition, and vision while remaining in a high state of alertness. He is present in his environment.

He registers all that is going on around him. He is conscious of his presence in such an environment. He is aware that his presence influences the environment. Furthermore, he is conscious that the environment influences him. Both he and the environment are influencing each other. He acts responsibly and respectfully to his surroundings. He understands that other presences or entities in the environment are also alert. Communication in such a moment and environment goes with senses and energy vibes. There is no room for verbalization.

The vibes and energy one sends out are what the other presences and entities react on. If the energy is friendly and peaceful, they will react back with such energy. But if it is aggressive and challenging, it will disturb the environment, and he gets back the same reaction. All this attention to being present and minding his place and his environment is a basic measure.

This is important for his protection. In such silence, he is alert to every other noise. When he hears the hissing of a snake, then he knows that there is danger and he prepares himself. When he hears a stick break or shrubs move without wind, then he has to be ready for any attack from an animal or another physical being.

The first thing he does is to alert his senses and focus his attention on the direction of where danger might come from. When he sees a crime being committed, his first protection is to sense whether he will be killed if he confronts the actor. If the actor is armed, then he has to hide and seek an alternative to escape without being noticed. Or he hides until the criminal finishes and go away.

If it is a crime he can confront, then he does it. Most of the crimes in the community that is carried out within such odd hours are reported by them to the community. Sometimes they will watch the criminal to see where he deposited the criminal evidence without the criminal noticing his presence.

When he sees a dangerous animal that can kill a person, he tries to make sure the animal does not see him. Although he has a very sharp weapon, he uses it for his work of tapping wine. He can also defend himself successfully with such weapons. Most of the palm wine tappers are also hunters and farmers.

In the odd hours, as we call it, the palm wine tappers and hunters also see other beings. Other beings that are non-human beings. Another word we use for them is a nonentity, to avoid mentioning the name when discussing them. These beings disappear when they see you first. If they are not aware of your presence, because hunters walk like predators, you'll have a chance of seeing them first. You often sense their presence before you see them. When you sense their presence, the best thing to do is to make a sign like coughing loudly. One can also make a sound like clearing their voice. The person can also whistle with the lips. What you do at that moment and how you react depends on what information your senses give you.

Your senses can inform you whether this is a dangerous encounter, for you to keep silent or let your presence be known. In that case, you can silently avoid the environment. But if your senses inform you that the presence did not expect you and will disappear if it notices human presence, then you will know for sure. Your senses never fail with right and safe information. The sense I mean here is intuition. When it comes to animals, it is clearer what you can or cannot handle alone. But for non-human beings without physical bodies, you have to fully trust your senses, especially your intuition. The sight, smell, feelings may deceive you because the entity can take physical form while it does not have one. It can also send a different odor than the one known for such an entity. Feeling ice-cold, tension, goosebumps, paralyzed and so on. Ugly, smelling like rotten egg or cadaver, but sharp.

Other kinds of smell that are surely not from nature can be perceived in the presence of such an invisible entity. Seeing fast movements that are difficult to register with your eyes and can disappear within a twinkle of an eye are signs the senses register to warn about other presences. For example, when you suddenly feel ice cold in a temperature of 40 degrees Celsius, warns you that an entity is right present close to you. When you have malaria, you can feel ice cold even in temperature above 40 degrees Celsius.

Your intuition will remind you to scan your environment so that you can be sure of what the senses perceive. Rationally, you have no clue how to deal with such entities. There is no training in this area. There is no study in these areas. There is no vocabulary to communicate with such entities. It is completely a non-rational issue. The non-body entities are non-rational and non-logical. You can never predict them because you do not know the power you are dealing with. You also do not know how they think. Their judgement and action can be extremely strange to the living. This is because they can judge with information they have that relates to you centuries or millennia before you. Judgement based on such information you don't have access to is impossible to comprehend. Spirits remains incomprehensible entity. Dealing rationally with them is assumed to be stupid approach.

With animals like snakes, you can take a stick to defend yourself or attack and kill it. You can also use a machete to kill it. Your rationality knows and understands what you are dealing with and how to do it. Therefore, you have information on those physical entities. When it comes to monkeys, running away is a safety measure because the monkey will chase you for a bit, turn back, and walk away. It knows you are afraid, and you are not looking for confrontation. This kind of information is stored in your knowledge. Rationally, you can access it and use it. Growing up in such an environment demands developing cultural understanding, knowledge, and wisdom of living in harmony with all of creation. The African's upbringing makes one pay attention to the spirituality needed in order to protect and maintain a balanced life with respect for all creation.

The area is full of beauty and danger. Both visible and invisible entities are entangled. They live with one another, both wild and tame. They share the river and the forest. They also share the nature and environment. Both are aware of each other's presence. In the lonely hours, the animals and non-body entities mingle around and carry out their activities. People consciously allow them to use their time unless they have activities to perform like palm wine tapping and hunters who use part of the same time. The hunters often hunt at night. They go in groups. You never hunt alone at night. This is because of dangerous animals that you cannot handle alone. Secondly, the non-body entities use the night for their activities. For your safety, it is not advisable to wander alone at night. Community or groups have more respect, and influence and are more protected than a single person. The hunters gather and move together. They are often highly equipped with spears, machetes, bows, and so on. They also turn on their headlights, like the ones used in underground mining.

When it is dark in the evening hours, they go off and come back before sunrise. In the dark, some night animals can be easily hunted with such light. Hunting during the day can be done without being in a group. Children are not allowed to go night hunting. It is only meant for adults who are well experienced in handling nonentity issues and nightlife. Africans used to say that spirits come out at night because they are afraid of human beings. The description of such an environment sheds more light on the African worldview and why Africans value senses more than rationality. Senses are the basic core of upbringing. Rationality is less valued than developed senses. Senses are the basic source of information and knowledge. Rationality is the process of accumulated information, understanding, and expression.

Chapter 9

THE STRUCTURE
OF THE AFRICAN WORLDVIEW

To get a glimpse of African spirituality, we have to mention certain important aspects. Africa has its own way of looking into creation. Their worldview does not differ much from many other continents, but there is still a little difference that made them have a strong bond with the spiritual world. The physical and metaphysical are interwoven as one. The metaphysical is a known reality. Africans believe that the origin of creation is God himself. He has the ultimate knowledge and also the answer to all questions of life and death. God is above all things. Every other thing, both visible and invisible, is under God.

A. Therefore, there is a God who is the Supreme Deity above all other spirits and forces. He is only destined for good. He is justice and nothing evil is to be found in him. He has all kinds of names that shows his position as the ultimate and highest of all powers every other power, both in spirit and physical, is under his authority.

B. Below him are other spirits and deities and forces. We call them godheads.

C. Under the godheads and forces we have ancestors.

D. After the ancestors we have the spirits of the dead.

E. After the spirits of the dead, we have the human spirits. The human spirit is the spirit of the living that enables them to enter into mysterious places, to go to the land of the dead of the spirit world, and to perform occult, magic, and some supernatural activities. This includes all born human beings, but also yet-to-be-born human beings.

F. Then comes the spirit associated with the personalities of other beings.

G. After which comes in the hierarchy the forces which are related to human efforts like achievements, good harvest, healing, and parts of the day like morning, afternoon, evening, and night.

H. After that comes the forces in inanimate objects which can be used to carry out activities of magic and so on. One can think about objects like a ring, and some religious materials and symbols.

I. As last on the hierarchy is the evil spirit like the devil which is incapable of good. Any spirit that is not capable of good belongs to the lowest in the hierarchy.

One can possibly cure an African of anything to the extent of reprogramming his mental and psychological components. One of the incurable components of African culture is his trust and faith in God. Culturally, Africans are incurable religious. In the hierarchy of African spirituality, we have the following structure. I will explain from the highest to the lowest in the hierarchy.

1. *God the creator at the top with the spirit realms.*

2. *Community follows behind including the visible and invisible members.*

3. *Family follows after with also the visible
    and invisible members.*

4. *Person (Individual) comes in last place
    but is the core and expression of the family
    and the community.*

5. *Things such as plants and animals have the lowest
    place but at the same time sustain human beings.*

Things, specifically animals, including birds and insects, plants, and inanimate objects and elements.The created animals and plants follow, including nonliving things or decaying and decomposing things. Nonliving things took the last position in the hierarchy of things. Things involve both spirit and physical, that is why I want to make it specific here. Africans have a specific relationship with things. The things of creation are part of all living things because they all come from the same source. The natural creation is spiritual, and its natural qualities are personally related. It means that those things in creation exist both in physical and spiritual realms and have a relationship with the person who is in touch with it.

The person addresses them according to his natural relationship with them. The spiritual realm of existence is a mystery. Some are treated as sacred because of the presence of spirits or gods in them. So, they are treated as agents of spirits or gods. Think about the elements that are deified such as land/earth, water, sky, light, sun, moon, wind, rain, cloud, thunder, darkness and so on which are worshipped because of their spirit. Their manifestation into being and passing away including all their activities possess some mysterious attribution.

Africans do not see these things as something a human being can take the form of or reincarnate into being. Therefore, their relationship with it is different from their relationship with human beings. Africans can conceive that their great ancestor's spirit or deity of their land can live in the stream or snake or tree and therefore they venerate such things. Because a spirit can live in anything it chooses as long as it is a living thing.

ANIMAL

Animals occupy an important place in African cultural views. They believe that animals have a sense of seeing and knowing that human beings cannot see or know. For example, a dog is believed to be able to see spirits. When a dog barks in the night, through the sound it gives, one can know that the dog has seen a spirit. When it is a thief or a human, the dog barks in another voice. When it sees a spirit, it does not open its mouth while barking. It growls very deeply and not very loudly. When it is another animate living thing, it barks loudly and even moves around. When it sees a spirit and growls, it warns the owner to be alert and not to come outside. Such exposure makes the spirit fear and it withdraws from the house.

They also believe that animals can detect poison. When food is suspected to be poisoned, they give it to animals to taste. If the animal eats it, then it is not poisoned. When they reject it, one can be sure it is poisoned.

When certain ants visit a dead body before burial, it is evidence that the dead man has committed an abomination or was an agent of the evil eye toward a fellow human being.

Animals are highly respected for their quality which people want to emulate. The most popular are the qualities of a lion or eagle or elephant. To sum it up, Africans have a relationship with animals that vary for different reasons.

PLANTS

Plants occupy an important place in African culture. Certain trees and bushes are sacred as living places for spirits and deities. Big trees like the iroko tree, cotton trees, and so on are special examples. Some forests are called sacred because of the presence of the spirit in them. It is also assumed that the herbal trees or leaves contain supernatural powers which are used for healing or carrying out supernatural activities. In other words, the spirit makes such herbs or roots of the trees powerful to act.

INANIMATE OBJECTS

The mountains, hills, deep valleys, rivers, seas, oceans, and such inanimate objects are the abode of deities and spirits. They are often scenes of sacrifices, locations for shrines, and supernatural events. Some difficult meetings of the village are done not in the palace of the leader, but in places where the deities are central in judgment and are ultimate witnesses of the agreement. Such a place evokes deep respect and awe. Whoever opens his mouth to speak knows fully well that he is speaking to the deities and not only to human beings. They will judge him. One cannot lie in such a place or carry out any form of deceit because the judgment is instant death or torture till death. Some of the objects are sacred or even medicinal. For example, when one eats poison and drinks water from a certain river or stream it will not harm him. When one is sick and bathes with water from a certain stream or river, he will be healed. Things like sand, alcohol, water, oil, salt, chalk, honey, cola, and so many others are essential ingredients of sacrifice or medicine, or magic. The priests, elders, diviners, medicine men, and the initiated members of the community possess the metaphysical knowledge and understanding of these forces.

RESILIENT

AFRICAN WOMEN

Chapter 10

COMMUNITY ETHICS
AND PUBLIC MORALS

Community ethics and morals are an expression of the structure. I will explain this briefly with the last and lowest in the hierarchy. This is because the strongest should be the foundation to carry all other ones. The strongest should not be on top. The weaker and lower ones will not be able to carry it. The stronger the foundation, the more it can carry. All things we can express are visible through ethics and morals. We will look into ethics and morals and then understand where it is coming from. The ethics and morals of Africans spring from their worldview and image of God, deities, ancestors, human beings, and creation. The goal of human beings is to be human in their role and place of creation. Ethics and morals are meant to help human beings be human. It forms the nature of human beings to grow into being human. Being human is a result of a well-cultured community where the person belongs. The culture of being human is not the work of the person only, but mostly the work of the spirit and community. It is impossible to be human in a personal effort. The spirit and community trim human beings' habits to being human habits.

Human beings are nature by birth with all its three contents of body and soul and spirit. The body has to go through many transformations in life. We will not elaborate on this topic. To make it short, the metamorphosis the body will go through is too much. Therefore, it needs to be well-checked. The desire of the body is often in conflict with the desire of the spirit.

The physical body of flesh, blood, and bones desires things like food and drinks which are vital for its maintenance and growth. The desire is often endless, which is expressed in many ways. Just to list very few like drunkenness, gluttony, factions, divisions, debauchery, hatred, envy, discord, orgies, jealousy, sorcery, idolatry, rivalries, impurity, rage, sexual immorality, selfishness, and many desires that make it weak to submit into slavery of impurity and wickedness. When the body is maintained with the desire as mentioned, it grows into a body of wickedness and evil content.

THE SPIRIT

The spirit is opposed to the desire of the body. The spirit desires things like togetherness, goodness, community, self-control, being good, intelligence, purity, love sanctity, wisdom, happiness, oneness, gentleness, brotherhood, understanding, freedom, being nice, peace, faithfulness, fruitfulness, patience, truth, joy, kindness, justice, and unity. When the spirit is fed with the desires, it becomes a slave to righteousness. This righteousness leads to love, wholeness, and holiness. Holiness goes with purity and freedom.

When you feed the spirit, you are bringing up being human, which is the call of the spirit in the body of a human being. Being human is a foundation stone for building a community that lives and communes together in harmony and peace. Such a group of people strongly living together as one, and sharing possessions and responsibilities together, is the call of all Africans.

Finding a balance between both spirit and body is the goal of upbringing, which is the task of the community. These are the goals of community ethics and morals for the well-being and completeness of the community. Everything in the cosmos is one because it came from the same source and functions in the same source. Like the body, soul and spirit exist in the same person and work in the same person. There is a cyclic movement in relation to all being God, human beings, and nature or other creations.

AFRICAN COMMUNITY & PUBLIC ETHICS

Community ethics and morals are the social expression of the structure. This cyclic worldview is the reason why Africans build their houses round. Their thinking is correlated with the circle of life. Things in nature are round, like the tree trunk and fruits and so on. The heavenly bodies like the moon and sun and so on are made more in circles than squares. The shape of the earth is rounder than squares. When you put an African in a square building or room, for example, it has a psychological effect on him. It is almost the opposite of his philosophy.

The seasons go in a circle. The year comes and goes. The rainy season and dry seasons come and go. The festivals come and go. The day and the night come and go. Human beings are born, grow old and die, and are born again. All this natural process is created by the creator to be like that. He loves the cycle of reoccurring and the structure of roundness.

The need or desire to have children is not only for economical reasons. The fundamental reason is to keep the circle going. The newborn is the reincarnation of someone who died at an old age and came back again. Nobody wants to be the one who breaks the generational circle of reproduction for the family and community. It is the responsibility of all members of the community to contribute to keeping the circle of life. Caring for each other is also part of this philosophy of keeping things going around. If you care for someone, that person will care for another too. It does not mean he will return the care to that person, but he owns a debt to care for someone else. In the relationship between the visible living and the invisible living, caring for one another is part of the circle. Life is a circle from physical to spiritual and from spiritual reincarnation to physical again. It continues like that in a vicious circle. Some of these morals and ethics are treated in the other topics. I would like to mention the issue of forests. It is an important part of the morals and ethics of Africans.

FOREST

Mary Slessor was a Scottish missionary who stopped the killing of twins around 150 years ago in my Igbo tribe in West Afrika. A twin was something strange. When a twin is born, then the family will throw the babies in the forest. The forest is meant for those people who do not fit into the community. It is for abnormal human beings. The forest is assumed to be a place of chaos. In reality, a forest is not a garden. A garden is a well-organized nature.

A forest is a wild nature that is not organized. It is a place of chaos. Africans have a way of using the forest both for metaphysical and physical living beings. It is a place where people suffering from leprosy were banned to go and live. A place for isolation and loneliness. Those who could not be part of the community or poses danger to obstruct the community lifestyle are sent to the forest to join the chaotic lifestyle. Living in the forest means you are not part of the community. It is a place for those who want to spread chaos in the harmonious community. An opposite of the inhabited community. In the community, the family lives together and keeps strong together. They pray together and work together.

They protect each other. The forest is just the opposite of it. The forest is the place where the body of one who commits suicide is thrown. He must not be buried. It is a bad omen and evil to take a life you did not make. It is believed that such an act is not welcome by God. In a real sense, the soul or spirit of that person cannot transit to the other side of living. He cannot join his ancestors because its time is not yet. He abruptly ends his life and there cannot go over to the next level because he is not called yet and no one awaits to receive.

He cannot belong to human beings' families and also not to his ancestors' community. He can only linger in the world. He cannot find peace. He will be restless. Such restless spirit causes evil and harms the living. This is because the ancestors cannot welcome him and give him a place to be at peace. Human beings cannot accommodate him because he has gone invisible.

The best place for such a spirit to linger is in the forest which is already in chaos and disorder. People who also died untimely are sent to the forest. Untimely transitions also mean that the ancestors cannot welcome the one and in the book of God the creator, the time for the death of that person is not yet. So, God cannot accept the person. The spirit will linger and will not be happy because they are afraid of what will happen to them and why they are treated in such a way. The spirits whose burials were not carried out as it is supposed to be done, for whatever reason, will not be accepted by ancestors. The only place they could go is to the forest.

The forest is for the wild and unwanted in the family and community. This is not only applicable to human souls, but also to animals and other creatures. One can fetch what he needs from the forest. It is a place to search for wild food, and it belongs to nobody. The only thing someone can own is a cash crop like big trees bearing fruits which one plants. But anything that germinates and grows in the forest is for all in the community.

Some forests are kept apart for the spirit. Which means not everybody can enter it. People like diviners and Juju or Voodoo priests are the ones to enter. The mediums who can communicate with the spirits are the people who lead someone or the community to those forests. It is assumed that one can only be safeguarded by them. They have contact and communication with the spirits. They know when the spirit felt disturbed or angry or when the spirit welcomes the visitor and what they demand to be welcomed. The role of the diviners gives them a respected position in the community. Diviners or mediums are important in sustaining and intervening in the well-being of the community.

In the forest, some rituals relating to cleansing and leaving evil behind are carried out. I will not go further into the kind of rituals done in the forest. Different African communities do different rituals in the forest. All the rituals are directed to the healing of a person and the restoration of peace in the community.

The spirit from the forest are the most merciless spirits. In the stories told by the women, most of the painful experiences are caused by the forest spirits. They are spirits of chaos, confusion, disorder, and restlessness.

TIME

Short story
Uchenna means *"God's thought"*

When I was at primary school, we happened to have a military regime that took over the government by sudden violent seizure of power. The kind of coup the military played to remove the elected democratic government and seize the governing power by force was not welcomed by the masses. The military decided to use force to rule. They applied discipline to all citizens. The discipline involved punishment if you fail to follow their ruling decrees and changes. The government institutions like schools and offices where civil servants work had to start work by half past eight in the morning. This was not new. It had been there for many years. The only change is that the vice president and some ministers would come to the entrance of the school premises or government institutions like the local government headquarters to await anyone who comes late. They will do this without announcement.

You never know where they will be. It does not matter whether you are working in the city or village. They will come with their whipping rope made of cow tail or rubber cable. Anyone who comes even a minute late receives some lashes. People started hasting and rushing to their work or school in the morning. Some could not take their breakfast because there was no time anymore. Nobody wanted to come late. Students and pupils ran with speed to school. When you hear the bells, and you are not already on the premises, then you know some lashes await you. Some old people could not understand what the rush is all about. They were told the story of the rules of discipline the military government established to regulate and guide the conduct of the citizens. They could not yet understand it. They asked, why should one run in haste to something that does not move or go away from you? In other words, why does one stress to go to work that is always there and does not go away? The word time coupled with stress is nonexistent. Running for time is very strange to African understanding of time. Punishing someone for time reasons like coming late is an act an African cannot comprehend.

Africans do not have clocks but they have time. Africans have their own time view.

Time is something that exists in our actions and memory. Outside our minds and activities, there is no time. In the concept of cyclic nature, things come back in their own time. The seasons come back. The day and the night come and go. The planting and harvesting seasons come and go. Giving birth and transitioning to the spiritual realm happens. Eating and drinking and sleeping and waking up happens. It is the natural creation of seasons that controls time. The festivals are controlled by seasons.

All the activities are where you find time in the African concept of time. Time is created by God in the season that controls activities. It is a phenomenon in the mind of a physical being. Outside the mind of a physical being, there is no time. The spirit devoid of physical entity is not attached to time. It is free from time. That is why the spiritual experience is everlasting. Everlasting is not for the physical body. It has expiring life. This expiring life is under time. Time in terms of the clock is nonexistent. The stand of the sun and light are used to measure time. Watching your shadow in the sun allows you accurate time to decide what to do based on what you need.

For example, if you travel to a distant place, and you want to get home before dark, standing in the sun's shadow will show you how late it is. You can decide whether to start your journey or not.

Some mental challenges human beings face are attributed to their understanding of time. Because time is in the mind, it can freak the mind and make it malfunction. A malfunctioning mind is like a forest. It is an abode of disorder and chaos. The misunderstanding of time causes anxiety and stress, which leads to many other problems. Therefore, Africans are not worried about the future because life is a cyclic issue and not linear. Most problems of human beings arise in the way one sees the future. The future is the main cause of pain and suffering. It is not the past. The past is gone. It is behind. It leaves behind the memory of the time of seasons and activities. It no longer exists. The recollection of it can be a source of desiring repetition of the beautiful experiences. It can also be that the memory of the past brings pain and beautiful lessons of life. The price paid for learning something you did not know.

The present is what one is always in. It is in the present that the past comes back. It is only what one has.

FUTURE

Uchenna means *"God's thought"*

There is no future because it is not yet there. It can never come. One can never enter it. Because it is never there and will never come. It is only in the mind and nowhere else.

I realize the truth in this when I was working in a highly tasking work. I was posted to a parish that was about to be closed because people were leaving, and the church community was decreasing. The remaining number of people could not maintain the big and expensive church building in the city of Amsterdam. I had secretaries and many people working with me. I created many activities and had also many people, even volunteers, working to achieve the vision I set up for my parish. Even my secretary who was very talented and hardworking could not manage most of my emails and I felt overworked. It was the first time that I longed for a holiday. That year, I bought a ticket to my favorite holiday resort. I was counting the days to go there.

Somehow, I was managing at work, looking forward to my holiday in that sunny resort. It was a treat I wanted to give myself and my young family of three children. Everything was arranged for them so that I could have a dream holiday. I still remember my last week at work before the holiday. Even though the workload was too much, I felt happy at my office. My mind was already racing to the beauty of that resort and the joy I was going to have. My workload at my office was no longer an issue because of the future I was looking to. My holiday resort was the future.

I arrived there and was really enjoying it. I forgot all about the work stress and workload. The sun-kissed my face and body on the beautiful beach. I had a great treatment. I spent some weeks there. My family enjoyed it too. When there was about three days left of my holiday. I remembered that I would be flying back to Amsterdam, to my work. I remembered the workload at my office. I remembered the stress and all activities. I felt down. I was not happy. It was when I realized that I was happy at the office because I would be coming to the destination I was at now, and here at that destination, I now remember that I will be going back to my office, and I was not happy. Still being unhappy at my dream destination because of the future I will be traveling back to. It then struck me that the future we are living in can cause a lot of stress, anxiety, and mental disorders. I became aware that it is not our past that gives us mental problems, but the future we are living toward in our minds. When one projects a happy future, joy comes in and the present is joyful. When one projects a stressful future, stress steps in, and pain or depression sets in. All this happens in the present.

Some people have this experience when they are going back to their home from a holiday or festival that was very nice. Such people, if their home is full of verbal or physical violence or both and tension, especially partners who are not compatible, might feel fearful and sad while traveling back home. It can be one of the partners who, after having good time, and is travelling back to a home full of negative energy and tension. The thought of going back there can raise fear and sadness. I have heard of people who sometimes spend some minutes outside their house thinking about how to survive the hours before leaving the house again. All these simple examples show how the future causes mental challenges.

Living in the present because the future is not in our hands and the past is gone, makes Africa time lethargic. Time does not have the power to influence people in such a way that it gives them mental challenges. What I mean by the time being lethargic is that time is not given that power over the people and the society. People who arrive from abroad, especially from where there is time and hassle, notice the natural relaxation in the atmosphere in Africa. This is the spirit that goes with such concepts. It is not the hot weather or things like that, it is the conception of the place, role, and use of time. Time is devoid of the future because the future does not exist. It is the present.

When Africans go to a psychologist who will start diagnosing the past to arrive in the present and then presents the future, it is a science that is meaningless to them. The issue of biography exists in the history of family lineage. What happens in your personal life is what the creation designed, which fits in the season of time. It is not wholly personal. It is in line with the activities designed to occur. One leaves the past where it is unless one has something to settle with the ancestors to restore broken or disordered relationships so that peace can reign.

FEELINGS

Africans are known as jovial people who sing, dance and smile, and laugh. This is a cultural expression of personal feelings in the community. Such expressions are often difficult without community. Expressing feelings, such as calling someone father is a sign of respect. When greeting each other some can bow down, kneel, or throw themselves upon the ground, kissing the dust with one's forehead and so many other forms. This courtesy is a sign of respect and love. It mainly reveals the dignity of the one showing courtesy. The one to whom the courtesy is shown becomes more aware of his identity and responsibility. It does not mean the one showing such respect is lower in dignity. It shows the honesty and expression of superiority and self-respect between both. Africans show little physical contact with each other. That is why they are not kissing or hugging each other with such gestures.

JUSTICE

Anuruekwube

The concoction Anuruekwube, which means to drink and talk, is important for truth-finding in my tribe. Living a righteous life is a call for all members of the family and community. This goal of life is transferred by each family member to their children and descendants. To be able to have justice, one cannot base only on trust that someone can say the truth. Truth is highly pursued in African communities. Justice is done by telling the truth. Anything that can help a person to say the truth is applied and allowed. Truth heals not only the person who speaks but also the one who falls victim to the act of the offender. The healing benefits all members of the community.

Because when misfortunes falls on someone, others who shares his joy also shares in the pain of misfortune. Searching for healing through the justice of the truth is beneficial to all families and communities who shares in the injustice done to a member. Truth reconciles the damage caused. This reconciliation is not only with personal relationships but also on a spiritual level. Offending someone or the community and telling lies is a painful offense to the community. It causes more damage to the physical and spiritual members of the community. Truth and confession are the tools for peace and reconciliation. Truth brings joy. Joy leads to peace. Truth is also doing justice to the offender and victim alike. Many African communities have a way to handle justice issues. The role of the spirit is standard, especially when the human effort fails to get to the truth. My tribe introduced a system of dictating any evil committed by anyone. This system was deemed necessary to help the offender defeat the feeling of shame, shyness and pride to speak the truth and set all free including himself.

This was a concoction called to drink and talk. Drink and talk, a specially prepared liquid mixture was used to force evildoers to confess all the evil deeds they committed secretly or openly. It is only used when someone willingly refuses to confess the truth. Especially when somebody turns out to be a pathological liar.

The confession is done in public in the presence of the community. When a crime is committed that has an impact in the community, crimes like murder which cause death, we will look into the effect on the community concerning the death. Crimes like robbery in a community, where there are no doors or keys in houses, shocks people because someone is taking what does not belong to them by force or in secret.

Giving poison to someone is also a serious crime because it can lead to the death of the victim. For any criminal act in the category of a heinous act, the drink and talk concoction is applied to get out the details of the crime. In such heinous acts, the community would like to find out and know the details. In some cases, it may not be a crime committed in the community. The crime can be committed by a community member elsewhere outside the community. It can also be that it was a group crime, where a member or some members of the community were involved in it together, or it can happen in a foreign country. If that crime is in the class of abominable acts, those members of the community who were suspects will be brought together in the community for public confessions. When they were gathered, if it is a group crime, the community will gather too.

Refusal to appear means not belonging in the community until one has gone through the ritual of truth finding. When all members of the community are gathered, the suspects will be given the concoction to drink. As soon as the person tastes the liquid they will begin to proclaim loudly, and with a loud voice and confess all the hidden and the visible evils they have committed. They would continue proclaiming loudly with detailed information, "I was involved in this and that" or "I did this, I did that". They will continue jumping up and down until they have confessed all the wickedness and evil acts committed. After emptying themselves of all the wicked acts, the power of the concoction will fade away. They will stop confessing. They will stop jumping up and down. They will come back to their senses and will become peaceful again.

If the person did not commit the evil act, and was just a suspect, they will not speak, and the concoction will not have any effect on them. If other evils in the class of abominable acts were committed, they will be confessed. But if it was confessed in the past, they would not confess it again. The spirit of the concoction never fails and cannot be manipulated or influenced. It is for dictating the offender of the crime and forcing this person to confess.

Public confession is a punishment in itself. It exposes an evil and wicked person in the community. Such a person is termed egoistic and self-centered, and does not consider the well-being of the family and community in mind. He isn't concerned about others except for his own interest even if it is to the detriment of the community. They are seen as a manifestation of wickedness. Public humiliation is therefore justice. This confession brings shame, loosing of face, showing that someone is dishonest and wicked. Such public humiliation, as punishment to the evildoers, makes them refrain from committing such deeds again. This method of dictating crime and forcing the public confession controls crimes and evil doing in the community. The community members are able to live upright and in trust. It works effectively in solidifying the foundation of the family and for the community to be pure, holy, and free from any form of corruption and wickedness. There is harmony and trust in the community. The members feel at home and in peace. They thrive together, live an upright life and live together as a family.

STINGING NETTLE / AKUGBARA

Because he was not conscious while confessing, under the influence of the concoction, another punishment is added. The public will understand that he is not punished unjustly and the spirit will know that the community did not let such crime go unpunished. The purpose of the punishment is to make him feel the pain he caused his victims and the community. He will not forget the physical punishment. After confessing under the Anuruekwube concoction, he has to be punished by staying under the midday sun, when the temperature is high.

A collection of fresh leaves called Akugbara is made, and some are squeezed out. Some waters of the leaves are rubbed on him. Some leaves are laid on him. The leaves are stinging nettles, or Akugbara, and they irritate the skin. He will also not be allowed to scratch himself. Tailor ants and soldier ants are left on him to bite him. He will not be allowed to kill them.

The community members do not attempt to carry out evil because of these kinds of measures.

DEITIES' ALTAR

Justice is sought at a cost, without loss of life. Unless in cases where the offender has to offer his life for the evil committed. In that case, there is another approach. When this kind of measure is not possible for whatever reason, or when the crime is more than the act in the category. The community will visit a deity shrine or altar. The deity can kill the offender instantly.

In such cases, it may be a crime that can be justified with loss of life of the offender so that harmony and peace will be restored between the ancestors and the community. In other words, the blood of the offender must be shed by the deity. No human being is allowed to shed blood without consequences. Ultimate justice of killing is not allowed according to the culture. There is no death sentence. Only God can give death sentence and carry it out himself.

HOSPITALITY

Africans are known for their open-hearted love and hospitality to strangers. An African does everything possible in his will for a stranger feel welcome at their home. Especially when the stranger is not an African or from his community. There was a story that a community killed a stranger who ran to that community for safety. The family, where this stranger ran to, did not protect him. He was killed. As a consequence, that family did not have a male child to continue the family tree. In another case, the family discovered in time that the stranger they killed was the reason of not having a male child. The stranger they killed was a male boy who ran away from slavery. The family was able to carry out the needed ritual. They started having male children again.

Another story was that a man killed his brother because his brother quarreled with his stranger. His brother had already discovered that the stranger came for an illicit reason to rob the brother. The stranger succeeded in robbing the brother afterwards. This last story shows how far an African can go in taking care of a stranger that visits. It also shows that they are victims of wickedness by those they show hospitality to. The tragedy they experience in their hospitality to strangers does not stop them.

The open-hearted love an African has for a stranger and the hospitality always offers the stranger the opportunity to know their vital secrets and can use them against them. In numerous instances, the African leaves the judgment to God and spirit realm to deal with the atrocities. It is often the final place an African sues his offender. It is the only place Africans trust for true justice. Sometimes it takes too long to get the justice done.

It can take scores of years. They believe that God does not judge instantly. In some cases, there is an instant judgement by God. An African can tell his offender, that he hands him over to the judgement of time. No kind of atrocity survives the judgement of time. Atrocity can be done for immediate gratification; judgement of time rectifies the atrocities through justice. Africans believe in such natural law that holds the harmony between the spirit realm and human realm in balance. Hospitality continues no matter how painful the experience may be. The good and the bad are entertained through hospitality.

Chapter 11

PERSON

In the African community and in public ethics, the place of a person is very vital. Knowing a person can be a synonym to knowing God. The person is the vital content of all the community and public ethics and morals. I want to use this reflection to introduce this topic of person. It shows that the image one can form about a person is never correct. It is a stereotype. Africans have to go down to their roots, which means going back to their generations, to have enough knowledge to access them. They never take you at face value, appearance, or your story. Let us see what one means when we talk of knowing a person.

A REFLECTION

The spiritual side of my being is correlated to the being of the other person.

God precedes me, and God's name precedes my name.

Who am I? Who is the other?

Am I the other, or is the other me?

The other looks and speaks from "I am", just as I do. We share "I am" in common. "I am," says the other, just like I say it.

When I hear and read all the thoughts, opinions, and images about myself, I wonder if it is true to who I am as a human being.

*If I search further within myself, I know it is not.
They are opinions and projections of others about
me and vice versa.*

*When I think about who I am according to others,
it is too much to mention.*

I am my name they call me.

I am also my body, my mind, my emotions, and my feelings.

*Anything I do with them is done by me. I am responsible
and I take responsibility.*

I am a father because I have a child.

I am a son to my parents.

I am husband to my partner.

*I am the culture I grew up in and sometimes
multicultural or dual cultural.*

I am religious thanks to the religion I joined or profess.

*I can also be multireligious because I practice
many religions depending on what I chose and
what is forced on me.*

I am African thanks to my roots.

I am my tribe thanks to my ancestral history or biography.

I am my nationality thanks to my nation of birth.

*I am also of another nationality (dual nationality)
thanks to my migration or naturalization or maybe
my parent's migration history.*

I am a specialist thanks to my working profession.

I am an academic thanks to my study.

I am a brother thanks to my siblings.

I am a friend thanks to my friends.

I am a partner, maybe in business relationships.

I am a colleague thanks to my co-workers.

I'm a man thanks to my gender classification.

I am, and so on.

These are a few examples of whom a person in social and work contexts can be. I am even more… Furthermore, my character's logical, moral, and spiritual qualities, can be made into an endless list. Such as:

I am loving.

I am righteous.

I am a person of integrity.

I am sincere.

I am open.

I am humble and so on.

But even with that, you can't say that you have painted a complete picture of me, as a human being and a person. More descriptions can be added to this, for example, of my skin color and all sorts of other physical characteristics of my unique being.

I am blond or I have Afro hair.

I am dark.

I am tall / short.

I am strong.

Moreover, that would be a long list. If I am talking about emotions and feelings, that is also a long list.

I am happy.

I am grateful.

I am sad.

I am angry.

I am, and so on.

But then again ...

No man is always the same, and yet he always remains himself. It is not possible to create a true image of a person. What Africans do when it comes to the image of a man, or a person, is to relate it to the community and the spirit realm. Any attempt to establish a person as an individual is a falsehood and lie. It is like an attempt to capture God in his image. No knowledge or understanding is enough to know a person and God. Let us look more into the image of man to see where it leads to.

THE IMAGE OF MAN

The notion that man and God are inseparable is a core belief. Seeing God, you see Him in man. Something of God is present in man, and we know that God has the last word of goodness, truth, righteousness, and love. Africans believe that man is capable of not being overpowered by evil. Through man, you see God and come to God. Things that seem contradictory in some cultures are not like that in African culture. This may be the most important message of this book. We will look into different topics that seem opposite to each other. Africans have the capacity of integrating such differences and also adapting to them and blending them all together in their culture.

An African can have in himself an inherited culture that is stored in his heart and mind. His mind recycles that culture and his body reacts to it. This is not his nature and true culture. It is actually a culture he does not want. The culture he wants is to be caring to himself and others. The culture of community life. To a culture that builds up lives and protects lives and properties. To be loving and harmonizing with creations.

Belonging to a community of union and trust. A person who is committed to fostering the well-being of themselves and others. His deep human desire is to be of service to others and to be loved.

In the world, as he goes through it, he faces challenges of the physical body and his spiritual self accumulated from the historical society and culture. He tends to react to this world culture. The desire to move away from the sickening culture to healthy and peaceful culture often gets aborted. Thinking about the story of the soul journey, this remains a challenge a man faces in the community that is transformed into sick culture. There are many circumstances that force the abortion of healthy culture and community. These circumstances are often personal and community issues.

I will take a few of them by looking into personal and then community settings. Both of them are our sources of life influences, and we live and die in them. Being conscious of it will elevate our chances to see and transform ourselves. These are issues of mind and body, individual and community, physical and spiritual. They are actually one and not divided. There is no dichotomy in African belief. What we call division are the components that make a whole. Imagine if our organs that work together are divided and separated. How can we function? The engineer of electronics and machines knows that components that make a whole function are often unavoidable. Our phone comprises different components to function well. We need wood or certain things to make fire for whatever purpose. When we dissect water, we can see different components of it that make it whole.

Our body comprises different organs and parts that make us a whole person. In that whole person, we are whole and complete to be able to function well and join as a body in a community. We need another person to fulfill a certain role to make a person more complete again, and so it goes on to form a community. Like two people coming together and having intercourse to make another person. They have something that must come together in other to make this third person a possibility. That is our true life. The individual is a component of different things that are supposed to be divided, but they are interconnected to make a person complete and function completely. The person as an individual does not exist. This is a deep core of understanding in African perception of personhood. The individual is not an entity. It also means the organs of the body cannot be treated as a specific entity. One organ is part of a whole. I mention this biological thinking because it has an effect on African thinking of health. We will see that all the thinking is one whole and cyclical. There is nothing fragmentary in African thinking.

Chapter 12

FAMILY

An African as an entity does not exist. An African exists based on the relationship with someone before him, next to him, or after him. An African exists in the plural sense. He exists in connection to someone or because of the other. He belongs to a social context of others. He comes to existence through the plural act of two people who worked together to make his existence possible. The social act that laid his foundation of becoming is not isolated, but part of the social acts of others. That is the basis of becoming a family. An African is confined to a family which comprises predecessors and those who are contemporary to him. He belongs to a big family of known and unknowns. In such a relationship, what happens to the individual happens to the community and vice versa. The individual can only exist in the context of the community. In a relationship with others, he can be conscious of his duties, his being, his responsibilities, his privileges, and so on towards himself and others.

He can only joyfully celebrate with others. He does not suffer alone, he does not rejoice alone, he does not get married alone, his wife does not belong to him alone, his children do not belong to him alone, his wealth does not belong to him alone, and his life does not belong to him alone. His death does not belong to him alone. His life affairs are shared with his neighbors, kinsmen, his relatives, whether dead or alive and some other persons. He is not alone. He belongs to a corporate body in the community.

The identity of an individual is only possible in a relationship with others. This is his service, self-awareness, responsibilities, and privileges. I can only be who I am in relation to others and vice versa. This is the summary of the African thinking of a man. Knowing yourself and who you are in relation to God, deities, ancestors, fellow family, and community members is the basic upbringing of an African.

He is the content of the moral and ethical virtues of the family culture to which he belongs. He will later grow to become a custodian of that culture as an elder. Knowledge to be able to carry out the responsibility of a wise elder is a lifelong training and learning process. The whole community supports him in the process.

There is no place for individuality in the family or community except in the plural sense. His existence is made possible by other people, including those he is sharing his life with and those of past generations. He is part of the whole. He is part of the whole body of the community, visible and invisible. It is the responsibility of the community to make and produce the person to be part of the community. Physical birth is not enough. The person must go through the rites of incorporation into the community. The child is born, but the person is given to the community to raise him and integrate him into the community. The rites continue from sometime before birth to the end of the person's physical life. The person has to pass through many stages of life, including the rites involved. The rites go on until that person dies and is incorporated into the wider community of the ancestor's realm and the physically living.

God created the first man as God's man and incorporate him into living with God, the spirit. God did not repeat his work by creating another man in the same way he did with the first. God took something from the first man to make the second. The first and the second are therefore connected by what is not visible. The man-made other person became incorporated into the social man and was brought to live in the community. It is a circle of creation that man is called to keep up. The social man is incorporated into the spirit realm through the rites of integration.

Whatever happens to the community happens to him. Whatever happens to him, happens to the community. An African exists because the community exists and because the community exists, therefore the African exists. To understand the African view of man, this is the cardinal point to start with. The African as an individual does not exist without the community.

He is not alone and is not supposed to know loneliness. A person is not a single entity in himself. He is a diversity by nature. A person contains the physical and material body which we described elsewhere. He also contains the spiritual that is immaterial entity which we described elsewhere. At least these two aspects make one diverse and not single. The interaction of this two in one being bears evidence that one cannot be lonely if both sides are in harmony. This also makes the issue of being in harmony very vital for Africans. Both the spiritual and physical are components and inheritance of generations before him who are present in him and in his world. The presence of those generations both spiritual and physical are felt by an African. He also takes a stand for them in his actions. Thereby taking a stand for himself. They are himself and vice versa.

The life of the person starts during the pregnancy, but the community life starts as a baby after birth.

NEWBORN BABY

After the birth of a new child, the umbilical cord and the womb are carefully buried in a hidden place so that no one can get it. It remains a family secret and only the mother and the father know where it is buried. This is done because when it gets into the hands of the evil one, he can use it to influence the destiny of that child negatively. There are powers within the culture to do that. In order to make sure the life and soul of the baby are secured, the parents carry out this security measure. The disposal of the umbilical cord and the womb is done before announcing the birth of the baby. After this is done, the man's family invites and informs the relatives, friends, and in-laws that a new soul is added to the family which is a good thing that happened to them.

The man's family relatives and married women will come together to the man's place. The child's father receives them and provides things to eat and drink, according to the custom prescribed to the gathered. There is always something specific that differs in different cultures which should be present. In some cultures, edible chalk, sometimes called edible clay, must be present for people to touch and eat. They will make a prayer and give blessings for the newborn child and its parents.

The women will sing and dance. Praise is given to God for the child added to their family. The grandmother of the child will come and stay with her daughter for some time. In that period, while the daughter recovers from the birth process, for her body to reset and all the biological processes to normalize, the grandmother of the baby will take care of domestic duties for her daughter. She will help her and guide her in taking care of the child and also of herself as a mother. She will also be monitoring the child both biologically and spiritually to understand who the child is and how to bring him up according to the need of the baby. The signs and expressions of the baby are cautiously observed to understand the message in it. It is a belief that a baby is a spirit that is pure and recipient. Because a baby cannot speak to communicate what it sees and hears, the spirit is free and open to talk to the baby.

Therefore, such verbal and non-verbal communication of the baby like crying, not being able to sleep, restlessness, abnormal marks on the body, expressing fear or shock, and any form of expression is taken seriously. To understand those expressions, the family has to meet a professional soothsayer, who will help diagnose the communication and hear from the spirit. Such an elderly woman, like the grandmother, has to teach her daughter the kind of knowledge needed to bring the child up to fulfill his soul mission.

CIRCUMCISION

Circumcision of the child happens after one week. The parents of the child will do the presentation of the child for this act of circumcision.

This is a ritual whereby the foreskin tissue of the male penis is removed by cutting. The female clitoris is also cut.

In both cases, the extent of the cutting depends on the local customs or the parents' wishes and the one who carries out the ritual.

Circumcision has different types for both male and female children as well as adult females and males. Adult circumcision is not common because most people get circumcised when they are children. In some cases, when someone is not circumcised as a child and it is discovered during marriage or interaction with fellow adults, then one can think about adult circumcision. Not accepting circumcision can have consequential effects on the person. It can prevent marriage or acceptance in the family of the person you want to marry.

We will not go into the types of cutting and the rituals involved in it. But we will consider why it is done, according to the reasons handed over. It is a form of initiation to the family, including the contemporary members and the ancestors. It is a religious practice. A kind of physical and blood sacrifice to the tribe. It is a ritual of passage from childhood to adulthood.

It is the means of curtailing a feeling of insatiable sexual desire or reducing sexual pleasure. It is a measure taken to have some control over strong sexual urges that leads to waywardness and sexual immorality which may bring suffering to the victims and destroy the community.

It is an aid to hygiene protection where regular washing of hands and bathing is impractical. It prevents the accumulation of dirt, germs, and bacteria causing other health problems. It thereby reduces the transmission of diseases.

It was a tribal ritual making a distinction between a circumcised group from their uncircumcised tribes. It makes the choice of a marriage partner easy. The circumcised marry the circumcised.

NAMING CEREMONY

God is the source of existence of a person and therefore precedes the person. A name is a spiritual issue. One cannot hold a name as one can hold a physical body or material. A name is what you pronounce or call out. Anything in the voice, words or air is spiritual by nature. A name is therefore spiritual. God is often present in African name because of his presence in the person. Therefore, giving a name has a specific approach. This approach is also spiritual. Only spiritual can beget spiritual.

It all starts during pregnancy. The family will try through a medium to find out who is joining the family. Which spirit is being born? The parents will try to come in contact with the baby before birth. The soothsayer will consult the ancestors of the family to find out about which baby will be born for them. In some cases, if this is not done during the pregnancy, it is done after the birth and before the naming ceremony. This consultation is important for the family for many reasons. The spirit or soul that has joined the family must be welcomed appropriately. The manner of welcome has an influence on the life of the person. Not all newborns are welcomed into the family. Some births are not celebrated in the family for certain reasons. In cases involving evil spirits in the life of the baby, either discovered during pregnancy or after giving birth. In this case, a certain appropriate ritual is done to protect the family and to prevent such from happening in the future.

Professional diviners are the people who will be able to give an accurate analysis of the baby. Such diviners are consulted in issues of babies and birth. This is because any form of false information or misguiding analysis and conclusions can have serious consequences for the life of the baby. The information from the diviner is needed for the family to know what to avoid, what to encourage, how to guide the baby during upbringing, the destiny of the baby, the signs to watch, and the family responsibilities. After gathering this analysis and information, a conclusion will be made by the elders of the family. If it is a satisfactory conclusion, then they will organize the naming ceremony. The first step is to incorporate the newborn into the family. This ritual entails announcing to the family the newborn's social and spiritual value to the family. This ritual makes the baby a part of the family. Biologically, being born in the family does not make one a member of the family. A newborn baby does not belong to the family unless he's incorporated by the ritual of acceptance being announced and celebrated. The incorporation is a thanksgiving to the ancestors and deities for allowing the baby into the family. It is also an act of blessing the baby in the family, both socially and spiritually.

The information acquired during the consultation by the professional diviners is used in deciding the name of the baby. The deity that is highly involved in the naming should be part of the baby's name. In some cases, the name of the deity comes first or last in a suffix of names that make up the first name. In some tribes, the deity may be Ogun (Yoruba in Nigeria) or Chukwu (Igbo in Nigeria) for example. The baby maybe called Ogunbiyii, meaning Ogun gave birth to this baby. The baby can be called Ezechukwu, meaning King God. Chukwubueze, meaning God is King. In cases where the ancestor reincarnates the baby, the baby can get two or more first names, whereby the ancestor's name is added. Those first names can be surnames after some generations. Names that are not from the family lineage or community are regarded as having a lost destiny. One cannot find his destiny if his name is not from the community lineage. It is assumed that you are born in the community because of the task you have to do for that particular community. The names as mentioned in the different stories of the women should be understood in this line of thinking. Names carry meaning related to them. The Africans who take a Christian name, because it is a criterion to become a Christian, do this by taking a European name. Often, they will have their African name as a second first name. The European will be the first name, the African will be the second first name, and the family name will be the surname. Name is destiny in African culture. The European name given to an African is often not used in the community. The community calls the person often the African name from the family lineage. The Africans who do not have a name from the family lineage are considered to have lost their destiny and identity. One of the worst things that can happen to an African is to lose his identity and destiny. Such Africans who refuse or reject their African names may be because they are not proud of it are often seen as one who hates himself.

DESTINY

It is not everybody that can carry out the naming ritual because there is a destiny attached to it. The name given to a child implies the child's destiny. It has to align with the soul of that child. The soul, being the mission and destiny, which is the reason for one to come into this world and chose the family, is determined by God the creator and sustainer of life. The personality of the child is determined by his soul. The soul is the direct link with God and it communicates with God, who guides it. The body is the house of the soul. It is the soul that makes the body and keeps it vital.

The ancestors are the spirit family members close to the soul to support it in the physical world. The ancestors and deities are responsible for the blessing and fortunes of the person. They give good fortunes depending on the acts of the person or family. They can also give bad fortune depending on the act of the person or family. Misfortunes are assumed to be a punishment from the deities and ancestors. Good fortunes are a sign of goodwill and blessings from the ancestors. In this case, there is not much space for the individual person to feel responsible for his misfortune. Hence, it is up to the deities and ancestors what happens to him. In this relationship and responsibility, the person has to do his best to keep the harmony between him and the deities. It does not mean that the person does not see his responsibility next to the ancestors. His responsibility can only bear fruit if the ancestors are pleased with him. Therefore, the relationship is tight and belief in a deity and also God remains intact. The soul has to undergo rituals both in good and bad times. It must maintain its relationship with God.

When a person's life is jeopardized and the family suspects that the person is responsible for that, a diviner is consulted to find out the truth. This becomes a family issue because each person's destiny is tied to the family's destiny. The family has to be together. The moral issue of the family should be protected. The person does not have to face the crisis alone. An individual's crisis is a family crisis. In interceding for the family, the hierarchy is also in its place. The elderly person in the family is entitled to intercede with the ancestors. In such a consult, the elderly take the lead to give permission or authority to others if he is not available. The firstborn son is the direct successor of paternal authority. The firstborn daughter is the direct successor of maternal authority. Both have authority that cannot be underestimated. The female authority is more than that of the male. The female authority has jurisdiction both in the physical and spiritual realms. In issues that the male members of the community can not handle, with things that are termed as crises, then the female steps in, and the crisis is over. Female authority can silence and stop the ancestors' catastrophes and other evil or crises in the communities. However, male authority cannot stand solving such a level of problems. Even in violent conflicts between people of communities, when women appear at the scene for peace, it is granted to them directly.

GOOD & BAD DESTINY

Having good morality and ethics protects a person's good destiny and assures that they will achieve the soul's mission. Good morality is security. God and the deities, including ancestors, stand on the side of good morality, blessing the person in return. Having bad morality is threatening to the soul's security and personal destiny. God and deities do not support bad morality. The morality the person chose to live with contributes to his misfortune, making the mission of the soul difficult. The character of the person is his major responsibility in modifying his morality and thereby his destiny. He must actively learn to acquire and practice good morality and character. The community's expectation and the person's self-awareness is important for his personhood. He should know himself in relation to others. The forming of his character is his responsibility. The community has all that it needs to support him, but he has to work on himself. A person's good destiny can be influenced by the ill will of people, evil ones and those who stand against him. Such person cannot be blamed for such outcome from an external evil influencing his life. When a happy destiny is changed by the act of evil to become an unhappy destiny, diviners and oracles are consulted to correct the unhappy destiny and turn it back to a happy one. In such a case, a consult by such a professional who will do the work is the option because the person cannot help himself against such powers. People maintain contact or devotion to diviners just to protect a happy destiny from the influence of evil who would like to turn it into an unhappy destiny.

When the person fails the responsibility of forming good character and cannot take his responsibility, not being able to function in the community, he can become a shame to his family and community. A person like such is sometimes sent out of the community or given to those who will take them out of the community to a place where he cannot come back to the community. In other words, people like that are sold to people from another tribe. This is done only when one has the capacity to participate and refuses to do that. When one does not have the capacity, the community takes care of him.

FAMILY

Family in African culture is often a large community with blood relationships. Each member of the family's life origin is known by reincarnation from the ancestors. The mission of life is foretold as well as the destiny of each member. The information can protect the life of each member of the family. It is often taken into account during the issues of marriage and death. In a situation where two people in the family bloodline are reincarnated by the same ancestor, when one dies, the other one alive will not see the dead corpse. He may attend the burial and all other things except seeing the dead corpse. In marriage, families with strong ties are considered even looking far distance in their history, maybe by many generations. As long the information can be traced, a marriage of two people with strong family ties will be avoided. The family ties have social impact. It regulates more than marriage or death. It also determines a person's social behavior towards other individuals of the family. Belonging to a family gives one a sense of home. It is the sense of family that forms the tribal life community. Family comprises of more than the living and the death relatives. It goes further into living animals, plants, foods, and non-living things, whether they are to be regarded as a concept or symbolic and representative of a particular quality.

Family is the core of moral development, while a person is the content of morality. It is the most important place to learn almost everything connected with human development. The concepts of life and living in human relationships, governing human behavior, habits, principles, thinking, worldview, and the whole life of the person in the community to which the family member belongs. It is the first foundation of life and living.

The upbringing is the responsibility of all family members in the community. This upbringing is not only the responsibility of the direct family but sometimes the whole tribe is involved. A tribe can be understood as the largest part of the society to which the family belongs. Tribe is a kind of family but with long lineage generations which forms their kind of world.

People have the notion that all Africans are from one family. Africans easily called each other brother and sister. This has to do with the sense that a family can be extended to be so large as filling a continent. It is a sense that because we have numerous cultural things in common, there is supposed to be a relationship traceable to link bloodlines. The notion that there is a shared past in territory, a marriage relationship, maybe in a long past the ancestors in spirit world living together and partaking in the relationship are things that some think.

In the family, the younger ones call elderly people especially fathers as father and mothers as mother. Even if the elderly is not your biological father or mother. It is a title of respect one observes for a predecessor. When people are the same age, you address them as brothers and sisters. Those who are older than you but are not parents or elderly, you address them as aunts and uncles. All the titles imply family relationships. This upbringing is the reason Africans address each other that way anywhere in the world. It is also the upbringing that makes them seek a community to belong to when they are in the diaspora. The notion of brotherhood is biologically and spiritually entangled in family ideology.

Family therefore is not limited to the nuclear one but extended to a larger one which comprises more. This is explained in detail in the community section. As I wrote earlier, African thinking is cyclic. Issues keep on coming back in different topics.

MARRIAGE

In Africa, marriage is an honorable event. It is usually a thing of joy for a parent to see their children getting married. Every family encourages its members to get married when they mature and become ready to enter into married life. Marriage is not an event between two people or to let the public know that they have chosen each other. It is a family and community event. It is an event where all members of the family, community, the deceased, the living, and those not yet born meet. When one refuses to marry under normal circumstances, this implies that the person rejects the family and community, and the family and community will reject him.

There is a dowry attached to marriage. A dowry is a material that the man gives to the girl's parents so that the parents can give away their daughter to the man. The dowry varies according to rites of marriage in the community. Some ask for a token and some demand many materials. The man may have to pay a certain amount of money. He may have to bring some things like a cow, sheep, lambs. He may have to do certain rituals, usually for the ancestors or the deceased of the girl's family. He may have to throw a party for the girl's family and friends or provide a special service for the family. It may also be that he takes in and raises one of the children in his home, and so on. All the things mentioned above can be demanded from a person as dowry. In paying the dowry, all the relatives of the man contribute something financially, socially, morally, or physically so that the girl is married not only to her husband but to her new family. This gives other relatives more right to say something when the man mistreats his wife or the woman mistreats her husband.

Moreover, when both are doing something wrong, with no attempt to improve, the other family members have the right to nullify their marriage and demand divorce. After the divorce, the girl remains a member of her family and is also a member of her new family. She then has two families. Her status in both families may be inferior, but her rights remain. She returns to her parents or family in case of abuse. Sometimes the dowry is repaid in whole or in part. The dowry plays an important role which can be the union of the two families, legitimation for the wife's children in her husband's family as a lineage, legitimation for the children to their father, a concrete proof of legal marriage alliance which is a kind of certification. Furthermore, when the husband or wife commits adultery, the dowry is proof of public accusation. The dowry serves as a thank you and compensation to the living and deceased who have contributed to the girl's existence and education. The dowry serves as a sign of appreciation for all the effort made by the family and community in bringing the girl up and showing her love. A dowry prevents a lady from going into the life of a man and becoming his wife without officially both families and communities knowing about it. It is a proof of the maturity of the man that a lady can be trusted to him.

Marriage is not an easy life although both partners in a marriage must reach the age of maturity before getting married. It is important for them to be able to take care of things when the challenging aspect of married life comes. He should be able to withstand them. Dowry gives the family and community of both partners the chance to get involved in helping them through difficult moments. Part of it is distributed to the girl's relatives, while part of it is used for the ritual of the deceased in the family. For example, if it is a cow, one of its ears is cut off so that the blood can fall to the ground for the deceased. The rest of the cow can be slaughtered for food or left alive for other material purposes.

In Africa, there is no category for single men and women. Any person who does not want to marry is considered a curse, a rebel, abnormal and all other bad associations in the community. Marriage is an important element of existence. The living, the deceased, and those not yet born meet in this agreement. The future of the descendant rests on offspring, since children are an important reason for marriage. A marriage without children is a failed marriage and can be a reason for polygamy. If you do not have a child, you are nothing. Therefore, the woman must do her utmost to have a child. If she does not succeed, there is an obligation of polygamy. The man is pressured by relatives or friends/brothers-in-law or even his wife to take another wife.

POLYGAMY

Polygamy is a choice when there are children born already. It is a necessity if there are no children born in the marriage. Even a widow can marry a woman or some women to get children for the family lineage. If the widow has only female children and no male, then he can marry another woman who can bear more children. He will continue this until a boy is born in the family. This is the primary goal of marriage, and also the reason for polygamy when it becomes a necessity. Polygamy is the act of having more than one wife. If it turns out that the man himself cannot have a child due to impotence or whatever reason, then he has a problem but still, it is arranged differently for example that another man helps his wife, but it will be a kept secret. Otherwise, the man loses his status and is considered inferior, because he needs respect to be able to lead and protect his family. The wife can also go far away and get pregnant without exposing her husband's infertility. Women carry a great responsibility in making sure that her husband has a child. A male child is vital in keeping the generation of the family bloodline of the man.

In some cases, if the family has female children without male, one of the females can get pregnant while at her parents' home and give birth to a male child. This child is often referred as an illegitimate child but accepted in the family. Thereafter, the lady can marry and continue bearing children with her husband's family. Most importantly is that the pregnancy of that lady which gives birth to the child should not be from a man in the house. Otherwise, it is incest, and that child will not be accepted. Accepting a child born out of incest will bring curse not only to the family but to the community that accepts such taboo.

The desire for many children often leads to polygamy. This desire stems from the problem of high mortality at birth. Other reasons are economic: many children also mean more labor to cultivate the land, thus increasing the economic wellbeing when the farming is cultivated manually. One needs more hands to produce more. The more children, the broader and longer the name of the person will live. Those who have children live and the more children the more likely to live longer. Life is carried on in memory or in a family tree. Polygamy is also a matter of prestige in the community; therefore, no one should have more wives than the king or traditional leader. Polygamy in the form of levitate marriage or widow inheritance creates women without support in a society where independent women are not tolerated. Caring for women in the community is a social responsibility. The deceased-living are dependent on the offspring, whom they make immortal through sacrifice and rituals.

When a man dies, a "levitate marriage" often takes place, and this is accepted everywhere in Africa. This means that the brother of the deceased man inherits his wife and that he conceives children for his deceased brother. In this sense, there is no widow or bachelor. Marriage is the default relationship for all adult women and men. Children are the most important desire for survival, physically and spiritually.

Polygamy is a justified solution for women who have no husband in a society where there are too few men and too many women. The nuclear family is involved in the life of every member of the family. This also includes the decision that are made in marriage. Most members of the family have an opinion when a member is getting married. This is because the member is not only getting married to one person, that is the marriage partner, but both families are getting married. It is a marriage between two families. It goes further to be a kind of marriage between two villages or towns. In both sides of the partners, both families have to get involved.

There is often investigation to know the full past of the families. It even sometimes involves meeting a soothsayer or medium who looks deeper into both families if the elderly people could not get to the root of both families. Any deformity or hindrance found in the process can be the end of the loving relationship. If the partners continue against the will of the family, then they become a non-member of the family and community. They have to start a new cursed family. Although this often never happens because the consequence is too much for one to bear. The hindrance for such marriage can be anything ranging from blood relationship in the past that is so strong that both families could not marry. It can also be that there is conflict in the past that involved a serious issue like bloodshed that is not settled yet. In that case, the family cannot go into union as one without settling their past. It can also be that one family is outcast that are meant to marry only from their family because they are offered to serve certain gods who own them. This happens in a culture where you have a caste system. Those who are serving the god, especially the god who oversees the community market, are called outcasts. Each community has a market situated at the center of the whole community under one leadership. They are specially chosen for that. Nobody from outside that family could marry from that family. Doing so is provoking the god they serve, which only wants children from the people offered to them.

These are just a few examples or reasons why an investigation is done in the spirit to avoid calamity afterward. Preventing such a relationship that will bring a curse instead of a blessing is necessary in caring for the family member. In different African tribes, different reasons are used to make sure that a relationship between families, both nuclear and community, is safe and blessed.

The history and attitude of the family are seriously considered in marriage. The morals and mentality of the family can be a reason to prevent the marriage. If a family supports stealing or are quarrelsome or with other kinds of morals that the culture or other family abhors, in such cases the marriage cannot hold. This has to do with the main reason for marriage, namely the procreation of children. The purpose of marriage is to have children. When a family is contaminated with evil as the culture terms it, then they will, through the children, extend such bloodline to another family. This is a serious issue that is difficult to treat. It is like bringing a curse to the other family by going into such union.

A marriage without children is termed a marriage that lacks blessings. Children are the ultimate sign of marriage blessing. Children are the assurance of the life wire and sustenance of the family life. This goes as far as sustaining the ancestor's well-being. An ancestor is dead when there is no one to remember them. Only the living members of the family remember the ancestors and keep their memory alive. When such a member dies and there is no one, then the ancestor is said to be dead. Ancestors have an interest in the marriage where children are born. Childless marriage is a big threat to visible and invisible life. A marriage without children is closing the door of the family history.

MUTUAL DEPENDENCE

Such caring responsibility is the reason African people share what they have with their families. One can travel abroad to go and stay with a family member who will take full responsibility for him or her. For example, in the case of schooling, one can travel to a family living in the city or country where she has to go to school. She will receive accommodation and full care from the family member at the expense of that family member.

In return, the student will take care of others too. This is the social and economic insurance the family has for one another. You share what you have with each other. Africans in the diaspora, even students, do their best to share their meager earnings with the families back home. It is a responsibility one feels for the sustaining and protection of life of other members. It ensures not only the status of the person in the family, but also to make sure the family and the people remain alive. It is a place to belong, and one has to sustain such a place.

If those people die, one has no place to belong. It has a long-lasting effect. Nobody wants to be responsible for the extinguishing of family life and bloodline, especially the death of ancestors. Someone is said to die if there is nobody to hold the name alive. The interdependence between the family is a responsibility for all to carry. For this reason, African people adopted polygamy to make sure children are born in the family.

HIERARCHY

The family hierarchy is not a choice of the family members, but the choice of deities. It goes back to the spiritual hierarchy of God the head and others under. God is the father of all human beings and the final point where everything goes back to. God is the beginning and also the end.

THE FIRSTBORN

By the virtue of the birth as the one who opens the womb in the family, he or she must be respected. It is a big responsibility to be the firstborn. After the position of the parents, the firstborn takes a position in the hierarchy. In some cases, the firstborn can overrule the decision of the parents in the family issues and take a stand against them. His position must be seriously looked into by the family or other kinship because of the virtue of being the firstborn and the responsibility attached to it. He or she is termed as the oldest member of the family outside the parents.

The parents cannot make decisions on difficult issues of the family without hearing his opinion. In numerous instances, he can overrule the opinion of his siblings. His opinion has a preference towards others in the family. He represents the family outside the family affairs. When the parents are no more, he takes over the family affairs as the head of the family among his siblings.

The oldest member of the family is a happening no one can change. The oldest receives respect based on age. If there is any share, the oldest has to take it first. In decision-making, the oldest has a veto. Mental well-being is often taken into consideration. If the oldest is sick and that makes his judgment or perception of reality incorrect, then the immediate junior in age should be consulted. In some cases, the oldest can wave his position and

delegate to his junior to make such a decision. In some cases, he can advise on what to pronounce. Respect goes from the oldest to the youngest. Another reason for the hierarchy is the status of the member. When a family member is chosen for a certain function like being the priest of the family altar, it is a medium position that demands respect. Respect is needed for him to exercise the authority he needs for the work. Without respect, no one can listen to him. Without the authority, he cannot perform the service of mediating between the physical members and spiritual members of the family. The intermediary role needs therefore respect. The same is applicable to the community leader.

This position is hereditary to generations of the family. The child of the firstborn will also take over his father's position in the lineage of the family among his extended family. During the community's gatherings to discuss the activities that concern the entire community's interest. Those who are called to the meeting are the opinion leaders of each family. These are the most senior ones in the family. When things are discussed at the highest level of the community, they will take it to their family level. A family can be a village or a few families that make up a village. In some cases, the few kindred made up a village. In any case, it is the most senior member of each family that represents them in a community gathering. The most senior member of the kindred family represents the kindred. The most senior member of the family in the village represents the village. The most senior member of the community represents the community when it comes to tribal community gatherings.

Therefore, it is essential to keep a record of which family and village, and community seniors the other. This information is very historical from the record of the ancestors. Any mistake in this structure can bring chaos to the whole community. Ancestors are assumed to be a community of justice. Any grievous mistake has a direct consequence on the living.

The issues discussed are taken to the family to be discussed by the authorities in the family community or kindred or village. The leadership will deliberate on the issue and give their opinion. If it is something to be shared, it goes through the same process. The most senior family member will take a share and will bring it to the family. The most senior of the family will take their share first, and afterward others will take their share. This structure is standard. Maintaining it keeps the family and community peaceful. When another structure is applied, the chaos never ceases until the original structure is restored.

This structure is why Africans see each other as brothers and sisters. Because, tracing it through history, they assumed that all Africans were one family. But because of the extension and family structure of leadership, they seemed far from each other. The spirit of family that belongs together from core family to extended family, which can grow to become a nation or continent, is a reality. This family is not chosen by the color of their skin or language. Africans have the capacity of giving birth to any skin color in human beings. Therefore, skin color is not a criterion for belonging to a family. Language is also not a criterion. What is mostly the criterion is acceptance. Because even the ancestors that one does not know and are never seen are assumed to be family and in reality, are served as a family. Africans have the mental and spiritual space to accept anyone as part of their family in their heart. They open their heart to truly love this person unconditionally. It is like a duty and life mission to accept someone in the community. This is cultural upbringing.

The most senior family member of the community is chosen to be the head of the gathering. In some cases, they are addressed as the king. The king leads the cabinets of the family opinion leaders gathering. He is the one who coordinates the affairs of the community in cooperation with others. If there is confusion about who is the most senior family, consultation is done by the deity of the community. The deity is the spiritual king of the ancestors gathering in the spirit realm. The deity will pinpoint the family who is the eldest. It is therefore intertwined working together with the ancestors. The past is significant.

The past is very vital to the present. Accepting the past implies to being at peace with the ancestors and accepting them too. Refusing to accept the past, means refusing to accept the ancestors. In doing that, one rejects himself because his existence is only possible because of the past. The pregnancy which formed him is a past. Anything that happened is termed to be in the past. It does not matter how long ago or how short ago. It is the past. Refusing to accept the past brings restlessness. This is because the relationship with the ancestors is not working. The ancestors who made mistakes have learned from them and are vibrantly willing to make corrections. They will guide the living to a successful life and show them what is valuable in this life.

Living in a balanced understanding between the ancestors and the living prevents chaos. The ancestors are there to guide, teach, nurture, and heal the mind. When the mind is healed, the chaos subsides. The community is the real place and ultimately a place to call home and to belong. It is the call of the African soul and life.

Chapter 13

COMMUNITY

Africans have a strong mentality of tribal or ethnic community. This mentality has always influenced national politics where different tribes form a nation, especially in a forceful act like colonization. The idea of tribalism or ethnicity emerges from a community-centered life. It is the basic social reality of human existence. Coupled with the incurable belief in God, the tribal community is created by God who is the author of all things both visible and invisible. This community is sacred and under the protection of divinities in different hierarchies. The divinities are ordered by God the creator to take direct care of the daily activities of the community. The ancestral spirits have the task of governing the tribe. Human beings have the task of maintaining peace and well-being. Both the visible and invisible have their task and work agreeing with one another for the community.

Both the visible and invisible are metaphysical realities and they respect one another. Integrity is maintained. Each must keep the promise of the other to maintain the covenant of that bondage. The goal of each human being is to belong to that community of your tribe and participate fully. Participation involves the belief, religion, ceremonies, traditions, customs, rituals, festivals, and other social activities. Participation is evidence of attaching yourself and being part of the community. Non-participation can be seen as detachment from the community.

It, therefore, means one is detached from social and spiritual security, foundation, identity, roots, sense of belonging, and existence. It is therefore a severe act of risking one's existence. It chooses a life of loneliness and a life devoid of religion, and an African does not know how to live such a life. An African without a belief in God is like a human being without a body. Detaching from your community ultimately means detaching from all the things that made up the community. The community is bigger than one can see or even imagine. It is a realm of human beings and spiritual beings combined. A link that has been since the first person in that community came to exist. All the dead people from that community remain as participants in that community.

In this community relationship, there is no death. It does not matter how many centuries someone died, the spirit remains an active participant in the community. This has to do with the African worldview of community and issues of life and death. In the African worldview, death does not exist. What exists is a transition from this side of life to the other side of life and vice versa. When someone's body expires, the person drops it like a worn-out cloth and transits to the other part of life called the spirit. The person joins the ancestors who do not need a body. He continues his work and commitment to the tribe and family. This worldview comprises a cyclic rotation. Life is round and goes around in a cycle. The spirit comes back as a human being through what is called reincarnation.

Such spirit comes back to carry out a certain task that is needed by the tribe. If the spirit fulfills the task well, it will return to the spiritual world in peace. Such a person who fulfills his vocation by doing beneficial work respecting the divinities and human beings is honored as a role model of a good life. His transition to the ancestral world means that he will continue such good work from there. It also means that he is more powerful in the immortal state of his ancestors. Transitioning from the human state to ancestral means transitioning from mortal man to immortal man. In that sense, there is no death, only transition. The cyclic worldview implies that everything that is natural is round. As explained in ethics. In life issues, cyclic implies that what you do on one side of life shall follow you on the other side of life. There is reward and punishment for the kind of life you lived. You cannot escape the consequences of your actions. This is because one retains on both sides, his human desires, emotions, feelings, and dignity. As an ancestor, one can show anger when the living in the community misbehaves and does not maintain the norms and values. The opposite is the case, if the living in the community maintains the norms and values, the invisible living (transited people) will be happy and give blessings to the living. I use the world of the invisible living to make a difference between visible human beings and invisible spirits.

The ancestor's role is broad. They act as mediators between God the creator, other divinities in the spiritual realm, and human beings. This is because they have an interest in the well-being of their family and community. In return for their services, they demand food and consumption as a sign of appreciation from human families. If such appreciation is not shown, it brings painful repercussions like the hindering of desired fortunes, hardship, pains, sorrows, sickness, and even death. In some cases, they can make everyone living in the family become extinct. Before they go over to punishment, they first give a series of warnings and messages through dreams, mediators, and appearing physically to be seen in a form that is not really threatening but unusual. In some cases, they will go over to make someone sick. When the body or mind faces sickness and the stress that goes with it, the person can feel threatened, and they will seek diviners who will explain what the spirits want from them.

One of the most popular words to express the community is the Ubuntu philosophy image. You are who you are because of the community that gives meaning and identity to your existence. Your existence is only defined by your relationship with others.

There are different kinds of communities that arise depending on tribe or ethnicity or how big the size of the community is. One has to realize that the notion of a nation is not an African worldview. Africa does not know a nation. Their original land map is tribal or ethnic. The land mass of the tribe is the land area for the inhabitants of that tribe. Within the tribe as a large community, one has clans, kindred, and families. Such divisions have to do with families that made up the tribe. A family becomes kindred and then a village and then a clan and then a town and then a tribe. A clan can also be as large as a tribe if the strong connection goes up to that level. The clan mentality can be created by the leadership structure. They have leaders chosen according to traditional birth rights.

LEADERSHIP

Each community has a story of its existence connected to a particular deity under God who is the creator of all beings visible and invisible. The deity has the spiritual leadership of the community. Human beings have a chosen leader who mediates between the spiritual and physical in running the affairs of men. This leader is chosen through the consultation of the spirit. The spirit chooses the leader and human beings give acceptance. The installation of the leader takes place in a great ritual that unites the visible living and invisible living. The main task of the leader is to maintain a harmonious relationship between human beings and the invisible living. The spirit is involved in choosing the leader because they know the secrets human beings cannot see. They know the person's spirit and spiritual realms.

They cannot be manipulated, intimidated, or dominated by a person. Their choice of that person is based on the morals and ethics embodied in that person. What is hidden from the human senses can be seen by the spirit. After consultation of the spirit and human beings, if each side confirms the person is eligible and good for leadership, then he is chosen. The leader must be good for both sides of the community. He must pose the qualities needed to keep the community's well-being. A bad leader is a curse to the community. The leader can be turned bad or wicked by a wicked spirit who wants to punish the community. This happens when the community fails to appreciate the spirit of service by offering sacrifices. The leader becomes a source of torture for the community.

Leaders go through extensive and complicated rituals that last for months and are carried out by different qualified specialized priests. After the priest has carried out the long lasting rituals, which are done in stages and mostly in secret, then the public installation takes place, which is often highly celebrated by the community. The small community leaders form the council of the tribe leader. I will not go into more extensive detail about the leadership issue because it does not have much role in the cultural issue of our topic. The important topics I treat extensively in this book. I would yet like to pinpoint that leadership is a very difficult responsibility because of all that is involved in it.

The head of the community is the guardian, the only guardian of their norms and values, their traditions, their identity, and their well-being. The head of the community cares for his people as a father cares for his children. He represents them, knowing that the spirit realm monitors and watch him. He is not only the guardian of traditions and norms, but he also embodies the human and world vision of his community. The community head stands for a coherent and accepted worldview. The signs that his leadership, whether he is called king or community head is accepted, is the well-being and peace in the community. All members of the community contribute their responsibility as one community to make sure the affairs of the community are well governed.

The leaders communicate to all members of the community by spreading news and calling for gatherings to discuss the affairs in the interest of the community. It is an oral culture, therefore many gatherings take place to discuss issues before making decisions. The town crier plays an important role in this communication.

TOWN CRIER

African communities have a news reporter through whom the leaders of the community spread the news to the community. He is called a town crier. He walks from street to street to shout and send out messages, warnings, news, and information to the people who live on those streets to learn. Each community has its own town crier.

He is appointed by the community leaders for the work. He carries wooden or iron gongs with him while walking about. He will beat it and people will listen when they hear it. Then he will proclaim whatever messages he has. He carries out his jobs in the evening after dinner, or early morning when the weather is cool and quiet. He has to do it when the people are at home without much noise to distract them from his message. He is the main messenger between the leaders of the village and the community. He can only do the job when the community leader gives him permission and a message.

Chapter 14

GOD THE CREATOR
AT THE TOP OF HIERARCHY

AFRICAN IMAGES OF GOD

Africans can never pick a fight with you because of the image or name you have about God. The trust in God is unquestionable. When I say African, I mean based on African spirituality and culture. The foreign religions that are politicized in Africa is out of the scope of my writing. I focus on African culture and not on foreign influences. The forming image is not necessary to the African in trusting God and godhead. Like in human image, Africans understand that any image about God is a human construction. It does not matter how perfect you work in creating an image of God, both in words and otherwise, God cannot be captured in an image. Our image of God can be compared to our image about ourselves and others. It is never complete and sometimes comes no closer to our own image. There are simply false constructions and perceptions of reality. All images of God and human beings are stereotype meaning false image.

The image of God that we have, makes influences in our speaking about God. We cannot talk about God in any other way than we talk about human beings or other creatures within our vocabulary and language. The image can never be complete or correct, and we therefore lack the correct vocabulary to speak about God.

African thought about God is a more socially related thinking. It is not strange because the African conception of life is social in nature. God meets people in balanced social and religious communities. Social behavior and morals say something about the person's faith. In other words, social life cannot be separated from religious life. That is why it is said that Africans are incomparably and incurably religious.

Africans do not believe in God, but do trust in God. Trusting God is based on their relationship with God. With your whole self, you apply yourself to perceive, with your whole self in solemnity, you feel, remain open, and let go of your thoughts, but also in expression with your body and senses. The African conception of God is not only masculine, but also feminine. This female and male concept is general to spirit. God, who is the origin of the human being, contains both in Himself. The image of God is difficult to judge what gender it has in different tribes in Africa. Africans have views of God where one could find extreme theism to extreme deism.

Africans also have many names for God. Africans trust in God the Most High, who is the creator. Besides this God, they believe in a crowd of gods who are under this God. Who have been and are working with this God since ages of ages. Then come other spirits of deceased people and ancestor spirits. Only then come the human gods. So, they have a pyramid hierarchical picture of deities. With God, the creator at the top and below that, the godhead, and spirits. Then the living, who are as mediators (medicine man/priest) between the visible and invisible. Africans have a monotheistic God. The fact that they mention many gods does not mean that they have many gods.

Ultimately, there is one supreme God. Believing in God for them means trust and total acceptance that for everything that comes to you, He is responsible. Without His permission, nothing can happen to you, total surrender to God who is the possibility of everything. It is also acknowledging His existence as beginnning and end. Nothing exists outside him.

African images of God as Creator, Almighty, Merciful or Gracious, Deliverer or Triune, and so on have to do with the personal trust relationship. God is Father, Creator, maker of life and the whole reality is inspired by God. He is in everything, and everything is in Him' (pantheism).

Africans express names of God that show how they relate to Him. Names like: Omniscient, Omnipresent, Omnipotent, Transcendent, Immanent, Self-existent, Pre-eminent, First and Last Cause, Spirituality, Invisible, Incomprehensible, Eternal, Unity and Plurality, Compassion, Grace, Kindness, Love, Comfort, Faithfulness, Goodness, Anger/Behavior, Will, Righteous, Justified, Holiness, Protector, Providence, Controller, Nurse, Healer, Deliverer, Leader, Boss, Judge, Leader in war (spiritual war), Friendship, Fatherhood, Motherhood, Source of Life or death and misfortune. Some names also correspond to the names of celestial bodies such as light, star, firmament, rainbow, wind, breath, spirit, lightning, thunder, cloud etc.

The image of God of the heavenly bodies expresses how God manifests Himself to them. That manifestation then becomes the image of God. There are other names that attribute different attributes and show different relationships with God, such as: Deliverer, Keeper of all, Big Eyes, and so on. Big Eyes is an image of God who sees everything we do and will open his accounts at the last judgment. Most of the names have influence in the relationship Africans have with the spirit beings. Pantheism, meaning God is in everything or everything is in God, shows the intimate presence of God in all creation and in the person. It is a different belief for Theism, which means God above everything.

Theism can have freedom from God involvement, but Pantheism cannot have such freedom because God is always present and is involved. Theism can put God aside in certain issues, calling it a dealing with human beings. Pantheism cannot have such thought.

SOCIAL IMAGES

Throughout the ages, African people have tried to make sense of the worlds in which they live and to form an image of them. African people try to put their worldviews into words. Their worldview determines how they respond to the natural and social events of their lives. The worldview makes life easy or difficult. It affects how they are in life.

In African society, the society view is determined by religion. African Traditional Religion is not a religion with a book and therefore there are no written materials. The community keeps the spirituality. It accommodates and tolerates other spiritualities and religions.

Africans have their specific own access to the physical and metaphysical society and worldview. It is only Africans themselves who can explain the heart and soul of the African continent. This is difficult for foreigners to understand. The metaphysical world is reality for Africans. In the invisible, you can understand the visible. Feelings of mystery and myth are always present in classical Africa, and these are still present in the African religious context.

African Traditional Religion plays a significant role in religious upbringing. In this religion-soaked worldview, myths and spirits play an important role. The Spirit has all the power and influences over the life of every person. A person or community cannot do much without the Spirit's permission. Man, and nature belong to each other and are at the mercy of the Spirit, whose power determines what direction society will take and how.

Therefore, the Spirit is consulted in almost all situations. In an attempt to have man and Spirit share power in a social order, one tries to manipulate or influence the Spirit.

This is done in the form of conciliatory politics, through concessions to religious leaders such as the priests and shamans/mediums. Africans are prudent in dealing with their world.

Because if you actively pursue your course and do not consider these social rulers (Spirits) it will mean that the Spirits will turn against you. The consequences of this will be terrible. So, these mythical stories and religious beliefs are the directional guide to the actions of Africans. Society exists in community with the visible and invisible. Both live together and are jointly responsible for what happens.

RESILIENT

AFRICAN WOMEN

Chapter 15

COMMUNITY & CREATION

Spirituality is a form of belief of being aware of the other dimension of human experience and personal connection with the spirit world. Spiritual awareness is where we as humans get our motivation in our connection to higher goals in life. Spirituality is the foundation of our education that forms our mentality through which we get the power in what we do. The power to have life, to love, for compassion, creativity, hope, gratitude, justice, trust, faith, care, to strive and so on. Our daily activities, including rest, often happens based on our spirituality. It is the force behind your waking up and doing what you have to do and going to bed to rest or for whatever purpose.

There are many things we do that we do not call spirituality, but it is all involved. There are many rituals that we carry out daily or in certain stages of our lives. I will list some here, but I won't elaborate on them. It is just to show that there are many rituals, which are well thought of for a purpose. The rituals include the following activities, namely brushing the teeth in the morning, dressing up, going to bed, waking up, birth ritual, and announcement of pregnancy. The announcement of pregnancy before conception often happens, but kept secret by the parents until close to the naming ceremony. In these specific issues, it is the spirit that comes to the family to announce it before the woman becomes pregnant. It is often a year or few months before the pregnancy takes place. The pregnancy period is also a period of both spiritual and physical preparation to receive the new member of the family.

In birth, the midwife who sees you first come out of the womb, before your mother and father saw you, has a role to play. There is a ritual done for this. The naming and circumcision rituals (welcome in the community) are social needs and the shedding of blood to the land. There are also rituals for the sense and for some organs in the body. There is a ritual for the newborn baby to adapt to sleeping at night and staying awake during the day. The touching of the stomach ritual is one of the most important after child delivery. This is done for the mother and the grandmother by the family of the baby. There are many other rituals that are not listed here. Rituals are used to support other natural courses like personal development and learning. Rituals imply that the spirits are involved to carry out their role in that area of life. nothing is left to physical process alone. Attention is given in both physical and spiritual aspects of the person.

COMMUNITY CARE ETHICS

One day, I was watching the planes taxi and park after landing or before taking off from the airplane. I saw some spotters near Schiphol airport, Amsterdam. One of them was standing next to me. We got in conversation with each other. He said to me, "I wish I was home. I wish I was in Africa. I hope one day one of these planes will take me home to Africa. I have never been to Africa. I left South America when I was born. My great-grandparents were brought there as slaves". "My name is Patrick", he said, as he continued his story. I looked at him and listened to his story and wondered what to say to him. I kept asking myself whether he understood what he was wishing. Being at home in Africa?

Could I tell him that I left Africa and long to go back? Could I tell him that hundreds of Africans are dying trying to cross the Desert and the Seas to reach Europe? Does he know what he calls home? After hearing him out, I realized the soul was seeking to be home.

During the corona in 2020, he joined a group of South American men and women who used all possible means to cross over to

Africa. It was an adventure of determined men and women. They sold their properties including houses and business. They started a farm with the money they made and the properties they sold. They are now well-settled and at home in Africa. Occasionally they will send me a picture or video clip of the produce of their farms and their environment. This gave me food for thought. He is at home in Africa, where he has never been all his life.

During my interaction with Patrick before his journey to Africa, I noticed the moral conflict he was struggling with. His soul demands a behavior that did not seem beneficial to him in the society he was born and brought up. He must follow the ethics of caring for himself, which contradicts what his soul needs. He could walk over dead bodies for his self-care as he said. He focused to get money even from the most wretched and poor in the society for his own upkeeping. That is the business world he was taught. There is no place for feelings is his pursuit for financial wellbeing. This are the norms and behavior code of business dealings. Though this was conflicting with his inner being and moral code, but he could not do otherwise. He was not at ease. During our encounter, he decided to choose a place to belong. His African soul remained intact and was in continuous conflict with the surrounding ethics of where he was at.

Understanding African ethics and morals helped him to understand the conflicts he was struggling with in his inner being. He understands where he fits in now and why he has moral conflicts. As he narrated from Africa, he has found home. He earns his money to maintain his upkeeping in a way that is no more conflicting in him. His soul is at peace. He is happy with his service that yields him a living. He belongs to a community that has history and identity. He is recognized, accepted, respected, and therefore he integrates as one of them in the community. His soul resonates with the environment and surrounding where he is. He is at home in Africa.

Living in a family and in a community-centered life is the goal and focus of an African soul. Africans have a soul tilted towards human relationships based on the ethics of community because their call is to community life. Being in a relationship is a very challenging lifestyle. A vocation of sharing your life without any reserve and secrets with someone is not easy. Sharing your life with uncountable numbers of family members, community, and tribe is not taken lightly in African culture. It is a life one chooses to be born in. One is not invited to join it. It is a free will of choice. What is done by the family is to incorporate the soul into the family and community life. Incorporation involves all kinds of rituals, ethics, and morals needed to maintain balance for all members of the family and community. There are many different kinds of morality and ethics. I will choose a few that are fundamental to the African soul and community.

The interdependence of communities and individuals in Africa has moral and social effects. Both affects one another. It is the individual who makes up the community. When the individual is celebrated by the community, they share the effects together. When the individual does something wrong that angers the spirit, the community is also affected. The community will make sure that the problem is solved. They have to go and appease the gods in order to restore the balance. This creates the moral idea that an individual's wrongdoing is the community's wrongdoing.

VIRTUE

The existence of human beings depends on the relationship between God, deities, and ancestors. Without these three bodies, human beings cannot exist. They all serve human beings. The main goal of human life is to live in communion and promote and preserve community life, physically and spiritually. Human life is sacramental and holistic. People who are born with a bad destiny can be changed through sacraments. In some cases, not all.

Those who are born with good destinies shall maintain it through sacraments. The whole essence of creation is for the human being. The spirit beings are there to support humans to take care and protect life and creation. This human vocation is sacred and needs to be fulfilled in the community.

In life, God the creator put His presence in all creation. Because they come from Him, He puts His guarantee in them. All created things have a purpose and service to render. They are needed and the Creator who has the ultimate wisdom made them. He did not make them to be wasted. As the author of Life and the one who sustains the living, He is concerned with His handiwork. He wants to secure what He made. In that sense, all of us in creation belong together. We reflect the presence and work of the creator. We are to serve one another. Our actions and non-actions are recorded and monitored. Both human beings and nature are at the mercy of each other. But we are more at the mercy of nature than nature at our mercy. If we spoil the air, we will die through bad air. If we spoil the water, we will spoil our life. If we spoil the soil, we will not be able to survive. The Creator gave human beings power over nature but he also gave nature authority over a human being's life. Nature has the final say over human life.

THE TREES & NATURE
GIVE MEANING TO EXISTENCE

Some trees must not be cut down because they pass water to the ground. Some give delicious fruits. Some plants have herbs for healing purposes. Under the tree, the community have their gathering and comes together to pray. With this kind of upbringing and knowledge, one develops an intimacy with nature. One starts to respect nature in many ways, as a manifestation of God and the ancestors. A tree is part of us.

The same goes for the animals. They are a part of human existence. They give us meat to live. One should kill one animal to eat and not two or more. It is the way to sustain each other as much as possible. When one kills two or more animals unnecessarily instead of one, it is an expression of lack of self-respect to man himself. The same lack of self-respect is applicable if he pollutes and destroys his environment. Animals and plants have a right to their form of happiness. For this reason, they may demand respect from us. We must give each other life to maintain balance and peace. We are branches of the same tree. Each branch differs from one another. Some are thick and some are thin. None of the branches must demand to be served by another or be respected without getting respect back. As children of nature, we are called to live in harmony with each other. This is the duty of every person.

We are in harmony when we can co-exist. When man fights nature, he fights himself. Because we are part of it. Being able to live sustainably together is the basic foundation of preservation and promotion of life. Africans have developed their individual and social morality from the relationship of the human body to other bodies, to nature. To live means to live together with others, including animals, insects, and plants. This is what you can call African spirituality. It is not a monopoly of humanity. Animals, plants, earth, hills, and trees are components of human spirituality. It is important to maintain the strong connection and lasting relationship between God, man, and nature.

ECOLOGY

Ecology is a dynamic concept. It is a way of life, an African culture of life. Man and nature are partners. From childhood, Africans are initiated to live in balance with nature. Africans know that it is wrong to disturb this balance. Disturbing the balance causes a total disorientation and spiritual disruption, which can also disrupt material life. When a culture loses its spiritual core, chaos ensues as people lose their sense of direction. In that case, one can experience the world as meaningless, which may make it easy for the foundation of life to fall away.

FORBEARANCE

Africans are often subjected to deprivation of access to basic resources to sustain their life or make the necessary changes. Living in such a dehumanizing way from generation to generation in almost every society of the world, he must have the inner strength to cope with things. The suffering that goes with such deprivation and degradation of his humanity makes him reach for his inner strength of forbearance. The belief is that he will overcome. Forbearance protects from despair and trains the heart and mind to endure.

Maintaining community life with different characters and habits of people needs patience and tolerance of others. Africans have a spiritual and open heart to accommodate others who are even opposite to them. The person you would never want to talk to or even see. Forbearance is a virtue that makes them socially create the space in their minds to allow that person in and even be hospitable. Forbearance strengthens the spirit of forgiveness. Enduring evil helps us to understand it, be able to see it from a different perspective and let it go. With a community-oriented lifestyle, each person is an embodiment of this virtue. Otherwise, community life will be almost impossible to remain in a home, to belong, and to fulfill your life destiny.

When someone turns to be wicked towards others and misuses his position to cause pain to others, he ends up destroying life and property. The family or community submits him to the judgment of time. One day, his body will expire, and time will bring an end to his evil. This means that the person can go on with his wickedness for many decades. The record of his doing will remain alive.

His children and those who supported him will suffer. People like that never reincarnate and stay alive. They often die as a baby or through miscarriage. Rituals are done to make sure they never come back to life to bring suffering to any woman's womb or family. Because such a soul suffers a lot when it comes back to the family. It brings responsibilities for the family members of another generation that did not know what he did to his generation. Forbearance helps one not to fall into avenging evil. The more you avenge, the more you add evil and suffering. Finding practical approaches to end such evil is where attention and energy is focused. Activities to make sure that life goes on even under unbearable conditions is the focus. While actions are taken to curtail the damages, evil keeps causing them. Concealing evil while working against it is part of the approach. Pretending that you do not know the evil action one is practicing is a necessary act of playing it low. Playing it low decreases the power of evil, showing that his actions have his expected result. One needs tolerance to withstand such a person for a long time. Forbearance is one of the virtues that made Africans stand all forms of hardship from generation to generation. The hardship caused in the atmosphere. The hardship caused by human beings. The hardships caused by the spirit world. In all of them, an African see an expiring date. This means it cannot always continue. One day it stops. It is this kind of patience with humans that keeps them hospitable to those who caused havoc in their community. They know very well who is wicked, but do not repay them back with wickedness. The notion that who wants something that is yours is a robber and thief and is lower than you is part of the wisdom of this virtue.

Giving and not wanting the thing you give back or expecting rewards helps in dealing with feelings of disappointment. When he is cheated, he concludes that the person is not dishonest and is not worthy of any trust. The person becomes worthless according to the African, no matter how the person sees himself.

Such moral conclusion helps Africans in dealing with dehumanizing conditions one can be subjected to because of the wicked and evil side of human beings. With forbearance, Africans keep on persevering, building, and keeping up the community life.

Chapter 16

BENEFICIENCE

A STORY UCHENNA

There was a story I heard when I was living in the monastery about how people live in Heaven and in Hell. The people have wooden hands. They cannot bend their hands. The table was full of food. They were sitting around the table opposite each other. In both Heaven and Hell, the people have the same setting and food and drinks in abundance. They were hungry but could not get the food in their mouth. The people in Heaven decided to give each other food. They ate until they were full and drank to their satisfaction. The people in Hell were looking at the food and drink, but they could not get it into their mouths and so they died of starvation.

There is a story that captured what I can say about the virtue of beneficence and how important this moral is in keeping life in an African community. It is the most cherished virtue among Africans. It is the heartbeat of the African community. It is the most serviceable moral that sustains community life. African communities are not assured in any way for life. Nature can be a source of disaster. People cannot store things for long. They are dependent on each other. Those who are strong carry the weak. Those who are wealthy share their wealth to make sure it serves others well. Those who can sacrifice their lives for the community do it without any hesitation as long as it serves the purpose of helping the community. In the history of Africa, many died giving their lives for the sake and freedom of the community. When I was a child, sometimes a certain spirit of a river would demand a human life in order to be appeased, for whatever reason given. The whole community would gather at the river and ask the spirit to choose whom it wants so that peace and freedom can return to the community. Such cases are often settled like that.

The virtue of beneficence is something one who interacts with an African will notice immediately. It is because of this virtue that an African can give a visitor his best, for example, food, and go hungry. He can give all his money and go poor and empty. He can give his bed to a visitor and sleep on the ground. Such act of hospitality or selflessness is not something you just learn at school. It is the core of moral nurturing and practice. It must be part of your being. People can misuse your charity and kindness or see it as inferior or stupid. Because you know what you are doing and you see their lack of understanding, but this will not stop you. You take their ignorance as giving gold to a pig who does not deserve it. It will not prohibit you from being merciful and compassionate. An African knows that doing good to others is a moral obligation that is not human law but spiritual.

Giving a gift is not buying someone or putting someone in your debt. It is an act of contributing kindheartedness. Africans live under the insurance of alms and aid from the community. The reward for beneficence is grace from the spirit. A beneficent person never fails to receive grace. A thankful heart and gratefulness go with the beneficent virtue. It is the most outstanding virtue in the African community. It is the core of the African soul. The opposite of beneficence is also the opposite of African ethics. Things such as savagery, cruelty, cold bloodiness, inhumanity, and hard-heartedness are some examples of the opposite of African ethics.

FORGIVENESS

The fruit of forgiveness is kindness. Africans cultivate kindness as a habit. With the goal of community life as the destiny of every individual, without forgiveness, the community cannot stand. To keep relationships, one must shun hatred out of his mind. Hatred is a heavy burden to bear and leads to prohibiting relationships. Without relationships, the community will not stand. Which means the goal of life and its destiny is a failure. Africans do not want a failed life. They work hard to make a living, no matter the condition they find themselves. The goal is to work and serve the community.

Human nature implies that human beings fail to do the right thing they are supposed to do. In such cases, people can be injured or face pain in social interaction or by someone who wants to injure them. The suffering brings separation as a measure of protection from more pain or suffering. This goes together with anger. Although, an African does not harbor anger for a long time. The reality is that separation increases suffering. Africans think about restoration in the other to reduce the pain of the person and the community. Bearing in mind that the African community comprises human beings and spirits, forgiveness must be sought by all parties who are injured in the activities. The spirit is also injured when the community is injured. Restoration to both parties go through the ritual of reconciliation that involves forgiveness. Both people can be reconciled if the spirit and the community are satisfied with the process and the outcome.

In cases where the offense is done in the community and has to do with the breaking of a taboo, the breaking of a taboo is one of the most grievous offenses in the community. Such a grievous offense that threatens the life of the whole community may require an ultimate sacrifice. A sacrifice that can be the offering of the life of the offender. It may be the only acceptable sacrifice to atone the spirit to come to forgiveness and reconciliation. When both human beings and the spirit are reconciled, there is balance again in the community. If there is no balance, one cannot conclude that forgiveness has taken place. There must be a check to find out if it is done.

RESILIENT

AFRICAN WOMEN

Chapter 17

WISDOM

HAPPINESS OR FLOURISHING (practical and moral)

Wisdom comes with age. It is a product of the accumulation of knowledge and understanding. Knowledge and understanding of the cultural environment and real-life situations are necessary to acquire the capacity for good discernment and right judgment. Self-knowledge is necessary for one to acquire wisdom. Wisdom that does not solve practical problems is not so useful for an African, especially when your goal in life is to have a community life. To acquire practical wisdom to solve practical problems, one must learn this from the tutors. The elderly are the containers of practical wisdom. They have an excellent pattern of thinking that leads to good decisions which bring the best solution to the community challenge. The discernment that hinders unwanted outcome or curtails it and enables good outcomes follows a pattern of thinking. Such practical solutions must have been proven workable in the past. People have applied it and know what works best. The elderly people who, through age and experience, had learned all the practical wisdom transfer it to the children. The children can apply practical wisdom at a young age like a teenager would if they had really spent much time learning from the elderly ones. Africans find it important to have their children spend time with the elderly members of the family.

In a community, there are issues the community can conceal until they find a solution to it. Exposing such issues may cause more damage to the community. One needs practical wisdom to discern such things. The opposite is also the case. There are issues that should be made public before seeking solutions. Otherwise, it may cause great damage to the community.

In African communities, we can speak about private and public ethics. Some taboos are treated, in ethical terms, publically if someone acts against them. These are taboos where the deities will measure out serious punishment to the whole community if the community conceals it. There is an adage often used here. Public sins demand public atonement. Evil structurally carried out for a long time against the community demands public hearing and retribution. It is not meant to punish the offender publicly, but to apply the right approach to such an offense. Practical wisdom is needed to have discernment about when public and private ethics are applied. Each application has the aim to find which kind of problem needs that solution. The practical application of wisdom must achieve its purpose.

Practical wisdom is the foundation of moral virtue to Africans. It is a necessary condition for good leadership. When a young person acquires practical wisdom, he is known by his use of words. He uses idioms and often speaks in parables. Such parables are meant for specific communication to a specific group or someone who is respected but should not be disgraced outright in public. But he has to hear what is said to him. Parables are used to communicate a message to someone who needs to change his way. It is to let him know that his act is not hidden as he thinks. A leader has to be able to communicate certain messages to a certain person or people in the community without exposing everything to everybody unless that which must be exposed to the other is to protect the community. Practical wisdom is a virtue that is highly pursued in the community. One acquires it in intergenerational community nurturing and tutoring. It can be applied in many areas of life. It is not only in serving the community but also in preserving nature and personal life affairs.

TRUTH / COURAGE

Truth is like a pivot where the whole foundation of African community life is founded. Every necessary measure is taken to arrive at the truth of the matter. No life is worthy of protection to sacrifice the truth. Africans believe that any life is worth being offered for the truth to reign. Therefore, being honest demands courage. People lie to cover shame and shyness. Telling the truth can make one vulnerable, especially when it has to do with someone exposing his fault or crime. A community cannot be strong and cannot be together if there is no honesty among them.

Someone who speaks the truth is respected and listened to. Truth often has the power to isolate someone in a community where lies reign. Africans protect the truth for the community. Therefore, whoever tells the truth is protected by the spirit and human beings, even if the person is an enemy of wicked ones who want lies and falsehood in the community. They are often in gangs to suppress the truth for their illicit personal interest. The community has a way to deal with them too. Such community action affects the person's family and generations. Some families are wiped out of existence because people believe that they will continue this from generation to generation. They are handed over to ancestors and deities, who will make sure that the whole family generation is wiped out. An African speaks the truth to free his mind from a load that tortures him.

IMPROVISATION / ART

African's natural singing, dancing, and rhythmic movements are not learned at school. It is born from a creative spirit of improvisation. It all starts in infancy. Many songs are songs sung to babies. While singing a lullaby to a baby, you carry the baby, sing, and dance. When the baby falls asleep, then you lay the baby in bed. Training the baby to learn how to sit is done with songs and dancing. This is also done when the baby is trained to learn how to stand. In this period, you will teach the baby how to dance. This makes it easy for the baby to learn how to move the foot and start walking. Dancing and singing continuously for the rest of their lives. The songs one sings to the baby are sometimes improvised stories. It can be anything you want to sing about. It is not rehearsed songs or specific baby songs. One has often to improvise it. In some cases, you sing and dance to the baby in sync with the spirit of that baby. You tell stories that the baby needs to know, believing that the spirit in that small baby's body is the same spirit that will be there when the baby is an adult. Though the spirit is in a baby's body, it should not be underrated as small or unknowing. It is an adult soul learning to use a body to grow.

Communicating to that spirit through songs, stories, dances, and many other expressions is found to be normal. The soul is enculturated in the rhythm of the art of singing and dancing. It is assumed that the spirit recognizes what is being done and is happy to experience it. The soul of the baby receives these songs and dances to soothe itself from communicated pains or questions to which it needs an answer. Songs and dances are soothing for the heart and soul. It makes the heart joyful and the soul peaceful through relaxation. A soul that is in terror and anguish can hardly express this with words, especially a baby that has no vocabulary of the language of the community. Self-expression is often by crying. The crying can be a message from a sorrowful soul or a frustrated soul because it cannot express itself.

This can lead to anger and upset, which is a normal human reaction when you cannot say what you want to say or get what you want, or when nobody listens to you. Singing and dancing express kindness and love. Such expression can console the soul. In a community where so many songs and dances are done, one must have enough to avoid boring repetition. Improvisation and creativity are necessary. The parents and grandparents, and in fact the community, sing to the baby. Then, at any age, as long as you can walk, you can join a dancing group from the village or community. Even the oldest elders have dancing groups. There are many festivities, sometimes all year round. Festivities without music, dance, and singing are unthinkable. Sometimes, some tribal or community festival prohibits singing and dancing of other kinds except the one associated with that festival until it is over. Such festivals last less than one month. Like many festivals, when I was around the age of five, I witnessed a night-waking funeral in my family. That was the first I could remember.

I was fascinated by how a woman led the women's group who sang the whole night. Holding her tambourine in her left hand and beating it with her right hand, she closed her eyes. I was told that closing her eyes keeps her soul connected and focused on the memories of songs stored in her heart.

She brought up a song, and the others picked it up and sang until they had enough of it. She knew when it was enough and moved to another one. She improvised numerous new songs that night, which others picked up and followed without practicing. She added numerous new songs to the families' songs. She sang from the beginning of the evening after dinner until breakfast in the morning. Her voice was still good in the morning, and all of them were in good spirits. They were not tired.

Improvising is necessary in an oral culture, where things are stored in the heart and soul. There are no written documents. No one makes any claim of ownership of songs and dance moves. Anything like this is for the community. No one takes credit for it. There is no market for it.

Improvisation is the source of African arts. This is not only in sculpture or painting and so on, but also in body arts like hair plaiting, piercing of ears, nose, lips, and so many other parts of the body. It is a creative spirit inherent in the African soul and practiced as a virtue.

FRIENDSHIP

This particular topic is easy to understand within African spirituality. The capacity to live in a community implies that one can easily make friends and easily socialize with others, even strangers. Friendship is the basic character and habit of socially relating with others. It is a habit to have a long-lasting relationship. An African becomes resilient with friendships, he can take much and accept much. He can overlook many pains and injuries the friend causes. It does not mean he forgets or did not understand or experience those pains as pains. He remembers the cheating, betrayal, deceit, and all forms of acts one can have in a trusted relationship. An African knows what is right and wrong based on his social upbringing and morality. But community vocation remains objective. Friendship is a character inherent to an African. Other topics like forgiveness are necessary to maintain the trust needed in friendship.

JUSTICE / HONESTY

African life is centered on two points that need balance for justice to reign. The community life that all members are committed to serving. Such service is just and is the goal of moral and ethical formation. The community has an obligation to the individual. Both sides must have balance for the well-being of life. In the quest for justice, human beings are not the only ones consulted. Deities are the Africans' court. It is an oral tradition that does not work with documents, papers, or any other form of documentation. When you buy land, you need just one witness while arranging the payment or exchange of land or property. In numerous instances, there are no witnesses. If there is doubt about whether this transaction took place, both parties are brought before the altar of a deity. The ancestors are called to come and witness. Both parties know that human minds can be corrupted and therefore can proclaim injustice. But such spirits, especially ancestors, do not lie. If they inflict injustice, then they are destroying the community themselves. Going to the shrine shows the need for justice. In some cases, the leaders will surely look into the case. If no one is sure if the issue took place many generations ago, then the elders have to resort to deities through a diviner. Injustice is something the African community cannot live with. If it is a stranger or non-member of the community that carries out injustice, it is another issue. In such cases, the consequences are not much for the community. If it is a member of the community, then everything must be done to get justice done. The actor of injustice can lose his life if he continues. Such death often carried out by the spirit/deities or ancestors are called justice. Sacrifices given to the ancestors and deities are called justice. Social services are called justice. Respect atoned to someone, or a title given to someone, are all termed justice and right. Rituals fall under the category of justice. Numerous activities are termed as justice.

RESPECT

This ethic is vital for community life. It is very difficult to be in a community where you are not respected. Respect is necessary for one to feel welcomed and a part of the community. It shows that the person is valued and has a place. Integrating into a community and participating in it is possible when respect is given.

African community life sees respect as a necessary condition for all members of the community. What is respected is not the physical body. Therefore, it does not matter what someone's body looks like. It does not matter how fat or thin, big, or small, long or short the person is. External appearance does not lead them. The African community is a union between the physical and metaphysical worlds. The spirits and deities occupy the highest place in the hierarchy. Human appearance is under the spirit. Every human body is seen as a house of the spirit, not made by human hands. Human hands make the human house. The human body is a house not made by human hands but made by the spirit for its home.

The respect shown to the spirit in a human body is not directed to the body, but to the spirit. A newborn baby is respected because you do not know the spirit of a baby. The spirit might be the liberator of human beings. Nobody in the community or family is chosen by human beings. It is the choice of the spirits and deities to join that community. Therefore, every member of the community is there to fulfill a task no other could fulfill. That is why everyone is sent. With such morals, each member is respected for the task and service he is called to serve the community. Without respect, it is almost impossible for them to serve. Respect implies acceptance. When acceptance and respect are fulfilled, the person can be fully integrated into the community. They can participate and contribute their talents and services for the well-being of the members of the community.

Clothing is an expression of respect. Each spirit deserves to be respected based on the natural hierarchy of the community. Clothing is seen as respect bestowed on the spirit of the other or others you are interacting with. It is not a show of wealth. It is an honor. Respect involves more than the above-mentioned expressions. Telling the truth and being honest is a mark of respect. If you respect someone, you will not tell lies to the person. Lies are seen as a mark of disrespect.

Self-respect is also part of respect. This is shown mostly in self-control. Treating others fairly is part of showing respect. Fair treatment is compulsory to maintain the balance and integrity of the community. When integrity is absent in a community, it will be difficult to maintain fairness and fidelity. Maintaining integrity to keep the community's soul peaceful, courage is needed to do the right things. Doing the right things demand respect to all and the courage to treat violation of the community's well-being honestly.

Chapter 18

RITUALS

A STORY UCHENNA

There were two big pots on the ground. Both contained edible things like chicken eggs, pieces of meat and so much different delicious and enticing foods. One was boiling, and the other one was not boiling. The twelve-year-old boys were instructed by the chief priest leading this ritual that whatever they can pick out of the pots, they can eat. Whatever you pick out is yours. We were never given such freedom to pick whatever we want in the public feast. It is always the elders who decide what you get and when you get it. This is a free-for-all invitation. All members of the community were present except female members. Those under the age of twelve were there too, except male babies. We could see that the boiling and steaming water was frightening to touch. The sun's temperature was about 28 degrees centigrade. It was still in the morning hours when we gathered on this square where the village has its altar for making peace with the land. It is called Ala Doro Obi altar meaning Mindful Peace to the Land. None of the boys dared to touch the boiling and steaming water.

What was strange was that there was no fire on any of them. Some boys went quickly to dip their hands into the pot with still water that looks cold. The one who tried first removed his hand before he could get hold of anything and shouted with pain. They removed their hands immediately without getting anything out. All men were quiet and observing. The edible things in the pot were really enticing. They are things you normally do not get often. Eating eggs is for adults. Those are eggs that refuse to hatch. Those were normally the eggs women cook for their husbands. Eggs are scarce; therefore, chicken owners are happy when their fowl lays eggs. They know that some will hatch, and some will not. You never know which one. One has to wait until the fowl finishes her process and takes the chickens away. The remaining ones you can take and cook. The more eggs that are hatched, the happier the chicken owner will be. It means more chicken and more money. In a few cases, the fowl may hatch all the eggs. As a child, you can hardly get eggs to eat. So, the boys really wanted to eat something from the pots. The first boy who tried boiling and steaming water discovered that it was ice-cold. So, they emptied the contents. We were baffled that the boiling water was ice-cold, and the still water was extremely hot. No one explained this to us. We kept on observing what other rituals happened.

After this part, the chief priest put a table on his head and turned invisible. We could hear him and see his movement through the table, but we could not see his body. Sometimes we would see the table fall and rise. We were afraid. We distanced ourselves from the altar and the pots because there was a serious battle going on there between him and some spirits. He mentioned the names of those spirits he was fighting against. There were some dead people from the village. He was calling their spirits for a peaceful settlement at the altar. These were the spirits causing some havoc in the village. They threatened the life of their family members and killed some. That was the main purpose of this altar. A place to make peace with the land. Both the living and the dead have to meet there every year to reaffirm that there is a peace agreement that each party has to keep. This altar was erected by the generation of my grandfather when they were young and were getting married.

SLAVERY

It happened that there were not many boys in the village. Boys were stolen at night and were sold for slavery. Another problem was that the women mainly gave birth to girls and not boys.

It happened that those males who were dead decided not to reincarnate anymore. They knew that their reincarnation would bring them to slavery. So, they wanted to avoid coming back to the family. Their life was threatened. Some young men were told what to do by the colonial white men. The white colonist lacked workers to help them carry out their work of colonization. A lot of them died because of the conditions and sickness they would face. They decided to recruit indigenous people to work for them. They would come and take a young man who was not yet married.

The community leaders were afraid to refuse their demands. The community leaders did not believe the white people were human beings because they did not see their feet. They were wearing shoes, and the community leaders did not know what shoes were. The white people were also enforcing their demands with violence if the community resisted. For that reason, many young men were taken. Some were returned after having training in the English language. They could carry out interpreting work and other activities for the white man to the community. Many of those young men did not come back. Well, the issue of procreation in the community was threatened in many ways. My grandfather's generation, who discovered what was going on by the forefathers, had to provide security for the boys before asking the forefathers to reincarnate for boys to fill the village again. Without boys, the village was destined for extinction. The spirits had to agree on whether the conditions and criteria were reached.

The ancestors were breaking the chain of relationships with the living because the living were not maintaining harmony. The living refused or could not protect the lives of the community. Instead of blessing from the ancestors, they are now cursing. Instead of assuring the future, they are threatening it. The most important weapon to destroy the future is to prevent reproduction and destroy children. Because the children are the assurance for the future.

When my father was born, his mother would sleep with him at night in a room with eight women. The thatched houses have no doors. It is a house built in a circle with one room and no windows. That was the normal building style. The only entrance door had no door to close it. This was why the slave traders would walk in the night and pick up the child and run away. They can walk into the room and overpower the young man and take him away. With their guns and other weapons which the community did not have, the community was defenseless.

The first woman will lie down across the entrance of the door. Another woman will lie down after her inside. The child will lie down as the last person close to the wall of the house. When the thief comes to steal the child, he must first pass the three women, they will realize what is happening and shout and attack them. Then the men will wake up and take over the hunt for the thieves. The women were the main protectors of children and life. This was how my father survived with his generation. His generation had many boys. Because almost every woman kept on giving birth until they can get a boy.

Ala Doro Obi feast is a feast of thanksgiving for the birth life in the village. It is celebrated every 26th of December. On that day, all parents who had a child that year will give a goat or fowl for the villagers to eat. I, together with other boys, used to kill the fowl, prepare the shed or tents for such a feast and gather the chairs. While girls used to fetch water and firewood.

Women did the cooking and dancing. Men prepared the drinks, killed the goats, and took care of other entertainment, such as music. It is one of the best days in December and in the new year period because all villagers have to come home and join this big family gathering.

All the killings of the animals were done at the altar by cutting the neck open so that the blood flows on the ground. The blood is what the spirit drinks. The people eat the flesh. When the killing is not meant for sacrifice, then the blood is collected and cooked in a special bowl with special herbs. The men eat this part of the meat. It is important for their strength and nutrition which they need for family responsibilities. This altar is the first place of the bigger family initiation ritual within the first year of birth. Even if you were born on the day before the feast, the family will bring the required gift for the community.

PURPOSE & POWER OF RITUALS

Every life exists under rituals that are found in the seasons and cycles of life. Rituals are repetitive in nature. The season is a kind of natural ritual in creation. It goes and comes back at regular intervals. The day and night including morning and afternoon and evening are regular occurrences. We have spring, summer, autumn, and winter which maintain their ritualistic occurrences.

The human cycle goes through ritualistic actions that bring about results. I don't believe it is necessary to go into more detail about the period from pregnancy to birth. When a child is born, there are certain measures that are taken in every culture. I will also leave this part aside because it differs in every culture.

A ritual is an action that you perform in a certain form as it is agreed upon. Participating in spiritual or religious gatherings are ritual. I'm not going to elaborate on that because every person has or knows rituals from their own upbringing or from others.

Rituals can also be like greeting someone when you meet the person first time in the morning. When you greet someone, you are greeting the spirit in that person. It is not the body you greet, because it is not the body that responds to you. The words that respond to you are from the spirit. It is the spirit because words cannot be seen. It is what you receive and perceive through the senses. In that case through hearing and sometimes vibration of the voice energy. Things that are repeated as a custom, tradition, or rite, not directed to material or physical are also rituals. Certain things directed to the material or the physical can be rituals as long as there is repetition.

A ritual can be brushing your teeth or taking a bath. Putting creams on your body too. Such things you do as part of your life. Some people find it hard to sleep if they do not pray. I mention it as something that is essential to our spirituality. The same thing occurs with customs and traditions.

RITUALS & SPIRIT

The spirit is the core of rituals. In rituals, you meet the spirit. It is a spiritual happening. A ritual is an act and desire we cannot neglect in life. It is just like going to the toilet. Something you cannot hold. You have to carry out the urge. The desire to come in contact with the other side of the world is a human desire. The door of coming in contact with the human and spirit world is ritual. The ritual opens the door for both humans and spirits to meet. When a human comes into the presence of the spiritual world, it is not taken lightly.

Calling on the spiritual world is accepting that we are human. We do not know how to do things as it is supposed to be done. We are weak. Therefore, before we take any adventure, we ask our spiritual partner to support or advice us. It doesn't matter what it is. Maybe traveling or working or starting a project or participating in a competition and so on. There is also a strong belief and faith that healing sicknesses and correction of misfortunes can only be possible through rituals. Such rituals cannot be copied from one culture to another. It has to be originated from the particular culture and the spirit customed to the people's culture. Integration of another culture's ritual can cause more havoc than being a solution.

THERE ARE DIFFERENT DIMENSIONS OF RITUALS NATIONAL OR TRIBAL DIMENSION

Some nations have certain rituals they do every year. Things like celebrating the harvest of farm products. The drinking of new wine or certain food crops. It can also be remembering the dead like people who died during the war. It can also be celebrating their Independence Day when their nation was set free from occupation or colonization. The saluting of the national flag is a ritual. The singing of the national anthem is a ritual. Each country or tribe or ethnic group has something that is done by all those involved in that group of people.

In national rituals, often important people who occupy positions represent necessary components and parts of the nation's organs. Such representation has a meaning to the ritual. It is binding to the community that formed the nation. The organs governing the nation are represented and therefore are bonded. It has a spiritual impact on all members of that nation.

COMMUNITY

Certain communities have their own rituals. During the community rituals, adults of that community are expected to be present. It is often meant to affirm the agreement of harmony and union of that community under one spirit. It does not matter what the spirit may be. I will keep this somehow general because this exists in different kinds of communities. In religion, the community is a known concept. People come together to affirm their belief and allegiance to a particular spirit. This is often the basic ground to participate in, believing in that spirit. It simply means all are bonded under the spirit. The presence of a non-believer in that spirit being venerated through the ritual becomes disruptive. This affects the harmony which the spirit expects. Such a person may negatively affect the ritual being carried out to that spirit. The ritual may not be effective or accepted by the spirit. Accepting the ritual is the main reason why the community carries it. It does not matter what kind of ritual is offered. It can be a special dance unique to that community. It can be a festival that the community celebrates together. It can be prayer and offers made to that spirit by the community.

FAMILY

Families can have a ritual that binds them together. They carry out the ritual together. It is often a ritual that is connected to the lineage of both the living and the dead. A family can pray together. Family rituals are often part of community rituals. The community rituals strengthen the family rituals. Both are connected or related because the family is part of the community. The head of the family is often the authority figure during the ritual. It does not mean that the head has to carry out the ritual, but the authority to carry out the ritual must come from the head. The family cannot replace the community ritual and vice versa. The manner of approach to both levels of spirit differs in both rituals.

PERSONAL

The personal ritual is part and parcel of the community and family rituals. All the rituals aim to ascertain the well-being of the person as a member of the family and community. Understanding the personal rituals gives more insight into the other rituals. In personal rituals, the person is moved to the act of the ritual by a personal motive with a certain aim and satisfaction. Something prompts the person to take the action. It is often an inner motive with external rewards. If the person refuses to act on such a need, it may have negative repercussions on him. To avoid such negative effects, the person is moved to act. The same is applicable to family needs for the ritual and the community but also the national need for the ritual.

There are daily rituals one may not associate with rituals. Things like taking your shower, cleaning your mouth and teeth, dressing up, praying, and any other acts a person carries out on a regular basis like eating are rituals. Things you do when you wake up in the morning or before going to bed that recurs are rituals. Therefore, rituals are not complicated things. You can term those things as your body ritual or personal rituals. Such rituals serve a purpose for your well-being and give meaning to your life.

Each ritual is carried out by those who are authorized to do such. This also means that there is responsibility for the one who is specialized to handle this ritual. Such responsibility is not taken lightly. A ritual is an act between the living and the spirit. It is like touching the spirit and calling its attention for a reason. The one who carries it out must know the territory he or she has entered or will enter. They have to know what the consequences of their actions will be for the ones involved. The person is called to carry it out in the name of the rest of the nation, community, family, or person involved. Any mistake has a painful consequence and carrying it out well has a reward. This hierarchy of rituals is intertwined with the well-being of all involved. It is hierarchy because if a curse comes upon a nation for whatever reason, almost all individuals in that nation face the effect. In that case, community rituals will not be very effective. The same thing is applicable to family or personal rituals. But if a person is under a curse, it will not affect the family, community, or nation. Therefore, there is a hierarchy of rituals. The personal curse may affect people under the leadership of that person if the person assumes a position of leadership.

SCIENTIFIC & RATIONAL CULTURE

Not all cultures respect rituals or recognize the power and roles of rituals. When culture turns scientific which arises by using rationality to dissect all things, rituals and their meanings are often reduced to be perceived merely as ceremonial. The spiritual meaning of rituals can be reduced to ceremonies that comfort feelings and emotions. Speeches and practices that evoke feelings and console are what such ceremonies try to achieve. The in-depth calling of a chosen spirit through a ritual act and communication is not what the rational person pursues. A ritual is something one carries out through the senses. A spirit acts on the senses. Approaching a spirit in other to communicate with it is what rituals aim to achieve. Ritual and belief go together. Rational and belief may be in conflict with each other. The same may be said of senses and rationality.

Rejection of the power of rituals in a scientific society has a serious effect on the well-being of the inhabitants of that society. Africans are brought up with rituals, but those in the diaspora lack the opportunity to nurture themselves with the sense of ritualizing their lives. This has a great consequence for their well-being. This is what prompted me to write this book.

Carrying out rituals without understanding the territory one is acting in may be disastrous for all involved. That is why those who carry out the community's or the nation's rituals must go through training to understand what they are doing.

We human beings cannot do without rituals. We have a natural need for rituals. Whether one believes in them or not, their power remains effective.

African migrants in the western part of the world instill the power of rituals in their well-being. Their migration did not disconnect them from the rituals and the ancestors' relationships. Some still have a strong connection with their ancestral roots which makes them homesick. Being in the civilized part of the world did not disconnect them from the ancestral relationship. The civilized society, with all its scientific development and culture, makes their spiritual life long for rituals. The scientific and civilized culture in which there are living things does not disguise rituals. It carries out rituals in public as ceremonies. It is the opposite of the aim of rituals. Rituals can be done in public as indicated in national and community rituals. Ceremony and rituals can be combined. Ceremony alone which is performed in the name of ritual has the opposite effect of the ritual. It does not bring the healing and peace ritual aims to bring.

The migrants prefer to disguise the ritual. A ritual is a form of prayer in which you have to pray preferably behind closed doors. It is your communication with the spirit that is hidden in secret. It is an act done to one in secret and to the spirit. To make this effective and safe, you have to meet the spirit in a secret and spiritual condition. When the spiritual act is done in public as a ceremonial performance without putting into account the spiritual implication, it causes a disaster that the participants can hardly imagine. In that case, it is better not to carry out such rituals than to carry them out with the wrong attitude. Being rational on these issues does not protect or make any difference to the outcome. It is a kind of natural law that does not make any difference whether you believe in it or not. Natural law works even against our beliefs. Spiritual affairs are natural phenomenon which does not ask for belief or permission to be and act. Understanding this issue makes those migrants from the culture of prayer and rituals keep their search for healing or solving their puzzles and mysteries through rituals in secret. In other words, they do not speak about it. The place of treatment is confidential, and the conversation is also confidential. Because all these things are done in secret and not in public, it is easy to misunderstand them. It is easy to think they do not seek help and that there are taboos involved. One can term them unreachable or not open for help. But in reality, they seek help in an environment that fulfills the criteria prescribed by the culture.

SECRET IN RITUAL CONSULTATION

African migrants and other migrant cultures who search for solutions in the spiritual world prefer to keep them a secret. In seeking such solutions, one has to meet with the spirit for help. The place of meeting the spirit is often sanctified and made pure and clean from human and spiritual entities that can defile it. A defiled space is not safe for prayer rituals that seek to achieve a solution. It will not achieve the desired result and it may even make issues worse because the spirit which is the core and purpose of the encounter will bring curses instead of blessings to those involved.

Sanctification from unwelcome entities or threats involves opposite power. The good power does not want to work with the bad power. The bad power does not want to work with the good power. Both are opposite and conflicting with one another. Those taking part in the ritual in the same space must agree with one another in the spirit they are communicating to.

AFRICAN DIASPORA IN TWO CULTURES

The civilized, rational, and scientific culture has somehow exchanged the ritualized lifestyle with the material lifestyle. As I wrote before, rituals have been reduced to ceremonies. As a pastor leading liturgy celebrations in a white community church, much attention is given to the preparation of the service. The order of the service is conceptually regulated. The procession is regulated. The music is carefully chosen to elevate the soul. The words to be spoken including the preaching are focused on elevating and regulating the soul.

As a result of the sometimes-strict regulations, especially for psychological and philosophical reasons, liturgical ceremonies can be boring for participants both young and old. It fails therefore to achieve its aim. Liturgy is a ritual. What liturgy actually aims to achieve for the participants is intimacy with the Spirit. The human spirit comes in healing contact with its creator and source. Such an encounter between the human spirit and the Godly spirit rekindles and revitalizes the human spirit. To be able to make this happen, the leader of the ritual must be in a state of grace and holiness. He must know that he is naked before God who sees his mind, heart, and thoughts. He can hide things from human beings, but here he is dealing with God who sees all things. A leader must bear in mind that when he calls God to come to the ritual, God will not be angry with him. Being in a purified state can make the ritual effective in working for those who attend it.

As Christian chaplains, our aim is to have this intimacy with God. In that intimacy, something awesome happens to the participants. There will be a feeling of fulfillment. Participants can feel peace and serenity. They may be feeling blissfulness. Healing, peace, and vitality are possible in such moments. These are what people are searching for in the liturgy. A place and moment to feel and be complete. Being and feeling complete is what liturgical rituals should aim to achieve. Participants want to feel redeemed and delivered from all the things that make them feel like they are in prison. The rationality and the psychological design of liturgy make it not possible to achieve those initial goals. The participants in the ceremony actually came for their spiritual need, namely communion with God, but sometimes end up not receiving it. To have communion with God, God has to be present. To invite God to be present or spiritually present, the criteria should be fulfilled before calling on that spirit. As pastors, we know the condition as liturgy leaders of the state you have to be in order to carry out the function effectively. A state by which the spirit of God will be present in order to work for the participants. In other words, God will come, participate, and answer the prayers of the participants. The leaders play an important role in this. If everything is scientifically arranged and carried out, it all ends up serving what is material and external, not spiritual.

SHOPPING

The effect of failed rituals or lack of rituals is the restlessness of a person or community. Nothing can fulfill the role and place of rituals in the human soul. Nothing can satisfy what rituals do to the soul. Everything given to man in creation has its own service which no other one can serve. People who lack rituals do many other things in search of fulfillment and wholeness. They can be addicted to other things in search of that fulfillment. Some urges will not be present if rituals are well done. Mostly, they search for solutions in the physical world and in consumption to alleviate the pain caused by what they lack.

They will go out shopping, drinking alcohol, using drugs, and giving out money and so on, in search of their desire and longing for peace. Those desires and longing are spiritual things that materials cannot solve. In the long run, a lack of peace will lead to other issues where the person will cause pain to others and the community at large. It can be done through a verbal act or violence. It can also be done through administrative acts. The person can use his authority anytime and anywhere to inflict injury to others. When restlessness and lasting stress lead to distraught, the person in question can freak out. A desperate and distracted person can carry out actions that no one can imagine or expect. Depending on the opportunity that person has, he can cause disruption to the community. The more power or authority the person has, the more he can cause disruption, even outside his community. This issue is applicable to any human being who lacks the wisdom of using rituals to make his spirit aligned with a Godly source.

FOOD FOR THE SOUL

The migrant who is brought up with rituals knows and feels ritual as true food for his soul. When there is emptiness and anxiety, he goes for spiritual feeding and communion with the spirit through ritual. When there is a sickness, he first thinks about whether there is a disturbance in his spiritual relationship. After a spiritual diagnosis, then he looks for a scientific diagnosis. In situations where spiritual diagnoses are absent, he will go for a scientific medical checkup or treatment.

The soul is always engaged in healthy and unhealthy relationships with the spirit. Daily I come across people and communities expressing ritualistic elements and beliefs. Some people do not realize what they are doing. I will therefore mention some of the elements as food for thought. Every human soul longs for rituals and communion with the spirit. Some are not conscious of it but they are daily desiring it.

Some people can hardly believe that wearing religious artifacts like a cross, an armband of saints, a rosary, a holy medal, or an artistic blessing works. Blessing or lighting of candles, the blessing of a home, the blessing of a child, the blessing of an adult, praying for the sick, blessing of a dead body, grave sprinkling for blessing, a sprinkling of holy water and salt all constitute an act of ritual and belief. The dividing line between faith, beliefs, superstition, magic, cults, folk belief, spirituality, veneration of nature and creation, or religious belief is a very thin line. It all depends on your angle of perception. The culture and community you belong to shape and form your perception of the other. All these listed show how different people and communities try to approach the spirit with rituals accessible to them.

One thing is common, all human cultures and human beings need communion with the spirit. All human acts to achieve this communion fall in the category of dubious practices. It does not matter the classification of the category. What matters is to recognize the need and the effect it has. The recognition will prevent the need or desire to suppress other people's needs of the soul. Suppression or denial of the needs leads to disorientation as mentioned earlier. The person can disintegrate from being human to a human being with the capacity to destroy others and himself. He will stop growing towards the call of his soul. Powerlessly lacking in spiritual strength and growth can lead one to seek fervently material power which does not solve the spiritual need. This leads to a person's lack of peace.

WORKING AND NOT WORKING

Do you believe in Juju?

Juju does not work unless you believe in it.

Do you believe in voodoo?

Voodoo does not work unless you believe in it.

Do you believe in the Evil eye?

The Evil Eye does not work unless you believe in it.

Those are all lies.

Things work whether you believe it or not.

My great-grandfathers prayed to their ancestors and honored them. They brought offerings to the lesser and higher spirits. As a Christian, I honor the saints but never worship them. I call to the angels, especially the archangels. I bring offerings to God through the church community to maintain my spiritual life. I am made to understand that Christianity is superior to the belief of my great-grandfathers. There is a change by truly looking at the practices. The idea is the same but the connection is related to what you are told and what works for your reality.

It all has to deal with ancestors who died. We still have a connection with them. They were concerned with our lives when they were in the flesh. They are still concerned with our lives in the spiritual realm. That is the idea of saints and ancestors. It is all in the baptism of the name. Does it work? If we call Christianity voodoo or Winti and still observe the names, rituals, and traditions we know, is it still going to work? This question remains food for thought for all believers. If Wicca is a lifestyle that works for their believers or other lifestyles, trying to destroy it by killing human beings is another evil altogether. Christians faced the same ordeal during the spreading of the gospel and still do in many parts of the world. In my country, they are still being killed daily.

The question of whether a belief works or not is irrelevant. The cultural problems Africans in the diaspora are facing regarding health issues can be termed psychosomatic issues. For those suffering, it does not matter the name given to it. What they need is a solution to the threat to their lives.

Our lives go through the process of healing, restoration, wholeness, the path to death and peace or paradise, or call it the path to ancestors. This is all we do in our community of faith no matter what religion you call it. A community of faith lays its foundation on the three levels of being. The three levels or kinds of being are the living beings, the dead beings, and the yet-to-be-born beings. This is a cycle that every member goes through in his life cycle.

Every member tries to find his or her place in it. This community requires two things that are material and immaterial. Material is commerce because you have to purchase things in one way or another. The immaterial is faith that you have within you. It is received in one way or the other and maintained.

My culture taught me as a child that, when I die, my family lineage will be there to welcome me. Even if I knew them or not, it does not matter. What matters is that they know me and will be glad to restore me to their community. My Christian belief did not teach me something different. The saints and the good ones will welcome me in paradise if I am able to make it to paradise where God has a big house for all people who served him well.

All notions are, that after life, you have a community to join. A community to belong to and life after death is described as a beautiful thing that no eyes have ever seen, nor ears have heard. Who would not want to have such an enticing promise? Christianity was able to force other religions in Europe to go underground with such a powerful promise.

Here is food for thought which I had been dealing with. As a migrant born in a distant country, I was brought up with different religions, languages, and cultures. My colonial language and culture are English. Leaving my culture and coming to another land and integrating into its culture does not delete my content or my culture. It remains in me. My connection with my ancestors and lineage is not broken. Regarding my connection with God, I believe it says that my God is wherever I am. He is with me always and everywhere.

Reflecting on this brought me to the issue of western religion that was abandoned for Christianity. Rejecting the European traditional religion to its opposite, Christianity, sacrifices had to be made once and for all. You do not keep on sacrificing that which has a lot of material cost and a lot of demand for daily lives. Were people set free from the bondage of the culture because a new religion was chosen? I think the answer is no. A lot of scientific possibilities are made to find answers to alleviate human suffering. We know that the material aspect is abundant, but spiritual suffering is also abundant. Science has taken the place that most rituals used to take. Yet it is clear that science is not the single solution to spiritual pains and suffering.

DEATH & FUNERAL

Like sirens, lamentations and wailing suddenly disturbed the silence in the village completely. From one time to another, tension and sorrow filled the air. It was a mix of different voices. Some were screaming, harsh sounds, and lamenting in many different ways. Some were very loud. All of them together sound like a crying choir that was carrying a magnitude of pain, sorrow, grief, and anger. The voices were like sirens alerting everybody that death had occurred. The women left all activities they were doing and they ran in the direction of where the voices were coming from.

Some held their breasts with their hands as they ran without footwear. They were running to join the chorus of wailing and lamentation. The more they gathered, the louder the voices became and the further they traveled to the neighboring villages and families. The community was grieving. The men were not running or going to the place immediately. Those who wear wrappers were dressed better in order to go out. They looked worried. The men heard the women's lamentation and were prepared for the ritual of consultation to find out the cause of death. They would find out who died. Children were kept at a distance or asked to stay home.

As a child of about five years of age, I did know that someone was dead. The only question one needed to ask when hearing the women lament this way is, "who died?".

This is the standard reaction to death and the first ritual when someone dies in Africa. It is the official announcement when death is pronounced. It does not matter how old or young, how good or bad, or what killed that person. This wailing is a reaction to death itself. Death is an unstoppable thief that nobody knows when and how it steals. But when it steals the body, often unannounced, the rhythm of life is disorganized. Agony takes place. The dying and the deceased have gone through agony and powerlessness. Emotions and feelings of not being able to choose whether you want to die or not or how and when to die are frustrating. It goes with a lot of emotions. Such emotions should not be rationalized or diagnosed. There is no fault on the side of the deceased. It is death that struck the person. The feelings associated with death must be exposed. Death must not be hidden but revealed.

When death comes and takes the body, Africans release the most powerful strength in human nature to react to death. That most powerful strength is emotions. Emotions are released in different forms. There are different emotions and therefore there are different forms to release them. They can sing, wail, lament, sigh, wave their arms, shake palms or fingers, sound, call the spirits, roll on the ground, walk helter-skelter, and many other ways to fill the environment with sorrowful emotions. Death had taken the joy of physically being and talking with someone. The body death consumed is given to human beings to interact with each other.

Death causes such an impact on the family, friends, the deceased person, and the community, that it must be expressed. The living has to feel it. The spirit has to feel it. The cause of death has to feel and see the pain it caused to all. Death remains a natural and unavoidable fact of life. One cannot deny or escape it. It is a fact that no one has any power over it. It can come in an unexpected process called sudden death or in an expected way called gradual death. No one knows who will be the next one the family or community shall lose to death. Such feelings of powerlessness are considered while expressing grief against death. Expressing the anguish and distress caused by death in a community brings healing to the heart and soul. The community that can cry together can laugh together. They can feast together. They can dance together. They can sing together.

Expressing grief and sadness together for many days is important for the living and the deceased. Separation goes with pain and grief. The living will accept that their loved one is now a spirit. They have to acknowledge this fact which helps them cross over and accept the separation caused by death. Through acceptance, they can let the deceased family go. The deceased will continue his journey to where death wants him to go. If the family did not let him go, he will be angry with the family because he cannot be either part of the family or part of the ancestors. With such anger, he can cause havoc for the family for not letting him go. This happens because he will be seeing himself as a member of the family, remaining involved in the family. Expressing grief and heavy emotions makes him regain the consciousness that he is dead and should continue his journey to the ancestors' realm. Grieving works two ways for the deceased and the family. This is why the ritual is very necessary to separate the deceased from the family and also to announce and share the pain with all who want to.

Expressing grief in such a public and loud way shows the deceased that he is no longer part of the physical body. Painful emotions are necessary to achieve the bodily separation between the family and the deceased. The anger against death helps to fulfill this bodily separation. Expressing this anger fully and with the whole community is a clear message to the deceased and also to the spiritual realm that he has to continue the journey to the ancestral realm. Without this expression of strong emotional feelings of grief, the deceased may be confused and still remain in the family. It may continue to intervene in family affairs or still hang around. He may communicate to the family without being conscious that he does not have a physical body anymore. As a result, he will think that the family does not listen to him. He may be angry and cause some problems because he cannot realize that he is dead. This often happens when the dead one did not see grieving people. When he sees it, then he will ask himself questions and then discover that his body and he are separated. When he tries to contact people and sees that they are grieving him, he will leave the family.

Grieving is the first ritual to fulfill the separation of body death caused. Grieving is also an expression to death that it is not hidden. Anything that is exposed does not have much power anymore. Death should not be hidden but exposed. Death is weakened when it is exposed. There is a belief that when death occurs, other spirits of death will come to see if they can take more lives. But with crying, lamentations, and heavy emotions, spirits will not dare to try to take another at that moment.

The community will at least have time to deal with the loss. Loudy expressing heavy emotions relieves the body of the individual and the community of the shock and negative feeling death carries. The anger of loss, the powerlessness that one cannot stop death and so many other things that cause emotional and physical distress can give way to some kind of relief. When such negative energies and feelings are released, the body will not store and keep them for long. The body will calm down. It will relax. They can talk about what happened and all the possible stories that might surround his death. This is the right of the community to know and discuss all the issues and to learn from them. Openly talking about it gives a feeling of togetherness and grieving together. It gives relief to a painful heart. Dancing and singing are part of this strong emotional relief. Grief is the expression of the negative energy stored in the body that came through the event of death, and you do not know what to do. This loss gives you such a feeling of grief that it does not matter whether it was a small child, adult, or baby. Death is death. It is brutal force and violence which awaits every living human being.

Lamentation and the expression of heavy emotions are the first rituals of the announcement. This is done by women whose special gift is to give birth to life. God and women have the secret of life and nurture. Death is the opposite of it. When a child is born, women come together to announce it with joy. When death strikes, they come together to lament against it with pain and grief.

After the first ritual of lamentation. The elders have the second task. They will gather and go together or elect a few of them who will go and find out the cause of death. This is done thoroughly within a few hours after the deceased is discovered. It should be done within one day. The cause of death is important information to make sure more death is prevented. Death is believed to be the work of God, Deities, and ancestors. It does not matter how death happens, whether through poison or accident, or long sickness. Even if someone commits suicide which is often rare, it is assumed that a spirit led him to such an act as an avenue to death. Death is only possible if the spirit assigns it. The last or visible cause, like falling from a tree, is the setup of the spirit to accomplish death. Sickness is the setup of the spirit to accomplish death.

Any known cause of death is what the spirit has set up to happen. The consultation with the diviner will reveal which kind of spirit and what went wrong in the relationship with the spirit realm. When someone dies at a very old age, diviners are still consulted to know the cause. When the diviner gives the information to the elders, he will also inform them what the spirit wants them to do in order to restore balance and peace. The person who died may not be the cause.

There was a case whereby a man was falsely accused of conniving and arranging with thieves who robbed a woman he was transporting. The man was a public transporter like a taxi driver. He was carrying only this woman who came for a family visit from one of the western countries. He claimed that he did not know the thieves who attacked them and robbed the woman. The community prohibits anyone from going to the police for any reason. Every case must be given to the community to take care of. She reported this to the community leaders. The elders of the village sentenced him to pay the amount back to the woman which the robbers took from her. The man felt unjustly treated. He paid the money. In his pursuit of justice, he went to find the truth.

He went to the shrine and called the deities to judge the case. The spirit went and killed the man who chaired the judgment. His death happened in less than five minutes. He was with his wife and family in the evening. He was talking with them in the evening moonlight just after dinner. He told them something hit him on his waist, but they did not see anything. He said it was moving to his leg and his stomach at the same time. He died immediately. The men gathered and went immediately to the diviner. The diviner informed them that they unjustly condemned an innocent man. The innocent sued them to the Deity. The Deity is giving him justice. The chairman of the community was now dead, and his vice chairman will follow shortly. All those who took part in the sentencing of the man will die. The Diviner advised them to look into the case again or else all the elders of the village will die. The man they condemned was not from the village, but the woman was from the village. On the same day, they found the man and told him what happened. The man confessed that he sued them by the shrine for justice. They begged him and he pardoned them. The same day they went to the shrine and withdrew the suit against them. They appeased the Deity. After that, they went to carry out the burial ritual of their dead chairman.

This story happened in 2020 and is to show that someone can die due to the fault of others. In this case, if the elders did not go quickly to find out, many other people could have died. This is why they always try to find out the cause of death and what should be done to protect the living. Speaking about justice, the woman also died after a few weeks because she falsely accused an innocent man which caused the death of someone. So, she has to also pay with her life. In such cases, the only thing desired to make peace is the blood sacrifice of the offender to appease the spirits. Not all mistakes can be solved with loss of life. The cause of death can be witchcraft, offending one's ancestors, God, or Deities. There is no other cause of death possible outside this list. Even if a human kills another violently it is the spirit realm that triggers it.

FUNERAL RITUALS

There is no known culture in the world that pays as much respect and attention to death as Africa does. The Egyptian pyramid with high-standard scientific building constructions and the mummies, embalmed to last for millenniums. Such technology for the preservation of dead bodies shows a lot of how Africans care about life after death. This is what they express when someone dies. It is not only a family issue but a community issue both for the living and the dead. The ritual is important for the peaceful and right passing of the soul to the ancestral world. The ancestors on the other side of the spiritual world partake in the rituals to grant the new spirit a peaceful passing. Just like a family prepares for the birth of a newborn baby and welcomes him into the family and gives the baby a place. Funerals are a basic approach to death.

The funeral ritual is not a ceremony but it involves very deep and spirit-minded activities. There are also funeral ceremonies that are more socially oriented with spiritual connotations. Both rituals, rites, and ceremonies take place when someone dies in Africa. It is all done accordingly. Rituals demand professionals who carry them out. The ceremony does not demand a professional. Making mistakes during rituals can be disastrous for the leader and the people even for the whole community involved. Funeral rituals have a specific approach for many reasons. Death creates a permanent physical separation between the deceased and the family and community. It is, at the same time, a gateway to everlasting life with ancestors. The rituals draw attention to this separation and life with ancestors and also make sure that the dead are not offended.

Death is like life, a rite of passage. Coming into life from the deep darkness of the womb to the world of light is a contrast. It is a journey without return. No newborn baby can be put back into the mother's womb. The passage is one way and there is no going back. Death is a one-way journey without return. Like the birth of a baby that is carefully done so that the baby does not land with a broken head on sharp objects or something dangerous. Also pulling the baby out or other activities during birth is carefully carried out to prevent any lasting injury.

Measures are taken so that the deceased is helped to make a safe journey to the ancestral world of spirits. The spirit realm should accept him so that he can have a community where he can be at home and at peace. The burial ritual is directed to achieve this aim. It is the right of the deceased that the living will work on. It is not only in the interest of the deceased that he will have rest, but it is also in the interest of the living. If the dead did not get rest, they may turn out to be a plaguing spirit. A plaguing spirit is dangerous for the family and community. It causes continual trouble or distress that ranges from economic destruction, ill health, family conflicts deaths, and anything that makes sure there is no peace and tranquility in the community. In many cases, if such spirits still could not find peace, it may be because the spirit realms reject to accept it in their community and the living has nothing more they could do. In such cases, the spirit is bonded and sent to the burial ground, desert, or forest. The spirit is restricted to come to the community. It will be restricted to going to another village. It is one of the worst punishments for the deceased. Holding the deceased by a tie or wrapping it with a chain to be able to restrict it by force is a harsh treatment. Such action is the way to expulse the spirit from the community. The spirit will never be at peace, but with such measure, it will not be part of the family or community.

Naturally, the purpose of life is to be accommodated in a community. Even a deceased person who died far away, the body or bones or any form or remains, if found, will be brought to his village and family to join the spirit realm of the community. This is done for the care of the soul to have peace and continue the service to his community. The soul is welcomed to stay home among the community.

Belonging to the ancestor's community is the goal of the deceased. From that community, one can reincarnate back to life in the family or community. The ancestors are the ones who prepare one to reincarnate. The burial rituals are very important for such a decision. If the family did not give a befitting rite acceptable to the ancestors, such a person may not be allowed to reincarnate. Not being allowed to reincarnate means being forgotten by the family. The name will be forgotten and that is true death in African culture.

This is the core of African belief in the cycle of life. The living is conscious of leading a life that will give them a place in the community of ancestors, which will make them come back again to the family. He has to face what he left while alive. In other words, what he sows is what he reaps.

A STORY

A man wanted revenge against his father. The man was not the firstborn of his father. His father gave most of the family land to the firstborn the reason was that the first did so much for the father. He took care of all the children of his father and built the house where all were living. He bought some land and built a house. He did not use his father's land for those buildings for the family. His brothers got some houses from him. As compensation, on his deathbed, the father gave him most of his land and shared the remaining among his two other children. Then the father reincarnates as the firstborn of the family to the second son. The second son was angry and told him that he will not get the right of the firstborn because he gave most of the land to his brother. He kept on reminding his son what he did to him in his former life. The story had it that the son decided to change position. He died suddenly and came back as the eight sons to the father.

When the father died, he was not allowed by the ancestors to reincarnate because of his revenge against his father. What you sow is what you reap both in ancestor and human realms. The circle is one. One cannot escape the consequences. Another fault of the man was that he did not accept justice done by the father to his brother. This is an example of why Africans leave judgement to the spirits. The time shall judge ones action whether it is good or bad in the eyes of the spirit realm.

Being in the ancestor's realm confers the person with more supernatural power. This power given to ancestors can be used over the human beings in the family. It is the power to bless or curse. The power to heal or to make sick. The power to save or to take life and so many other powers over human beings. This is also why the family or community cares for each other. When one dies whom, you cared for, he can give you blessings instead of curses.

The deceased maintains his body in the spirit realm but with the capacity to move around and carry out activities like ancestors. Being an ancestor is the goal of the deceased. The burial ritual is necessary to assure this position and reach the goal of joining the ancestors. If the goal is not reached, the deceased will not achieve the desired goal of joining the ancestor, which is the goal of all individuals. The spirit will become a vagabond who cannot find peace. The chance is big that he will hold the family responsible for his unhappy situation. This may lead to harming the family to force them to give him a befitting burial.

There are some important criteria to make this goal easier. Living a meaningful life is necessary. One must add meaning to the family and community life where he belonged. Although contributing to the life of other people outside the community is highly welcome. The moral of being good and contributing to life and living is highly welcome. The family that gave the first love and nurtured the person expects something back as gratefulness to do the same to others. One should do this while alive, knowing that the ancestors will check his record of service and judge him on the possibilities he had to do well for the family. Based on the outcome of the judgment, they will allow or reject him. They will reject him if he did not show gratefulness for the life and love the family gave him.

This judgment or one can call it criteria, is not written anywhere but in your own conscience. We will see more of this upbringing that forms the conscience in ethics. The point is that there are no criteria taught on this, but the culture of hospitality and care is present all around in the family and community. When you receive with joy then you know that giving is also joyful. Being stingy and selfish is a choice one can be harshly judged on when meeting the ancestors.

Committing suicide or having your life cut short is an offense that no one can accept. It is an abomination to life. One cannot take a life he did not make and cannot make. Life does not belong to man but to God. Life is spirit. Taking what does not belong to you is stealing. That is why death is a thief. Taking your life or the life of others is an abomination. Such a person is ostracized from the family and community while alive. If the person is too influential to accept this severe punishment, the family and community isolate them and officially exclude them. It means anyone who associates with him or visits his house receives the curse laid on that person.

The exclusion of the person from the family and community is also what the ancestors do in their realm. When someone commits suicide for whatever reason, the family and community will not give him the right to a befitting burial. It is already concluded that the ancestors will not receive him. Giving him a befitting burial may bring a curse to the family or community in general. This is because it is assumed that the family supported him and should therefore be under the same curse the person brought to himself.

There are possible rituals to accept that person back if he can fulfill it. This ritual may demand an exchange of life which is carried out by the deities and ancestors. In other words, the issue will be brought to a deity who can decide how to take the life. No human can take a life for whatever reason. It is the deities and ancestors that kill someone according to their verdict. In the case of the one who took his own life, there is no ritual that can be done by a human being and no judgment. His fate is left solely to the ancestors. Deciding to end life no matter the circumstance is never accepted or even discussed by Africans. It is taboo.

Long-suffering in sickness that leads to death is seen as a chance given to the person for reconciliation, making peace, and saying farewell to the family and community. It is a great opportunity to carry out the necessary preparations needed to be admitted into the spirit realm of ancestors. Africans prefer therefore lingering deaths that come in a natural way. Even if the death is caused by the hand of his enemy for example through poison and so on. Lingering death gives the opportunity to tidy up any mess made in life. Death that happens outside old age or matured age is termed premature and unnatural. Such death is suspected to have an evil connotation. The obligation each person has to the family and communication which is central in upbringing in African culture makes this issue of life and death decision impossible for the person to decide. In cases where one will prefer to end his life, he will leave this decision to the family or community. The outcome can be assured that it is not even an issue to be discussed. It is taboo to talk about. Therefore, the person cannot take the decision to the family or the community. Such a decision is left to God. This is also applicable to unborn babies.

Committing abortion is part of this taboo. You cannot kill an ancestor who decided to come back to the family is the notion. You never know why he is coming back and what service he has to bring to the family. An unborn baby is a soul that should be loved and nurtured and surely accepted until otherwise is proven.

The reality of physical death is known to Africans but not death as the end of life. Death as the end of life is not recognized by Africans. Contemplation for death is not encouraged or accepted. It does not matter if it is their own death or the death of others. This taboo makes it difficult for a young person to talk about his will or discuss how his property should be shared with the family when he dies. Africans have an oral culture, therefore the issue of writing a testament or will does not exist. There is an oral will that is as strong as writing. Sometimes it is even stronger because the fear of the spirit is involved and they heard it, making them witness to act on someone who breaks it. The written one is assumed that the spirit does not read and therefore getting rid of the document is being free from it. This is then in modern Africa with the foreign culture of documentation which is not part of this book.

In an oral will, a person who is advanced in age often makes the request to allow them to die in their own room or in his shrine where the spirits of the ancestors are present. In circumstances where the person is living abroad or is admitted to the hospital, he tries to be back home to his room to die there. Such a moment will give him time to communicate well with the ancestor's realm who will be receiving him. They can inform the children where they want to be buried, because of land issues. They can point out necessary things that should be done if they cannot speak anymore and could not die.

SHORT STORY

For example, that something somewhere should be loosed or untied or a sacrifice that should be made. There was a man who could not die after many weeks of being in a coma and breathing heavily once in a while. It was clear that he was supposed to have passed away weeks before. He said farewell to his relatives and was prepared for the journey to meet his ancestors. He was still breathing but his body was decomposing and smelling. There was no external wound. People knew that his inside was decomposing. Only he is still breathing once in a while. The family noticed restlessness and stress in the family. The man was already appearing to some people as a spirit giving them a message to share with his family. The family was urged to see a diviner to enquire about what to do.

When a diviner is consulted to find out why he is not dying or not dead already. It happens that he already told the family what they should do in such cases when he could not speak anymore. He made a pact with a deity that he should not die a sudden death. The pact involved that something he hung somewhere in his room should be brought down, otherwise he cannot give up his spirit and breathe his last breath. When that is brought down his soul can be free for the journey. It happened that his soul is tied in that. His family remembered that he said it, but they were afraid to participate in bringing it down which may hasten his death. They did not want to be involved in taking his life. The diviner told them that he was already waiting at the gate of the ancestors and becoming angry about why the family was not letting him go because the ancestors refused to let him in until the family let him go. He could not be on both sides. He could not come back to the family. He had passed from the realm of human beings to the realm of spirit. He has passed the gate of no return in the spirit world. There is no coming back. He is therefore stranded in the world between both human beings and ancestors. A special diviner was called to come and bring the bag containing the pact down.

He breathed his last at the same hour and gave up his spirit. The restlessness in the family stopped the same day.

This kind of will is common among those who are mediums and reached maturity age. In such cases, someone can be let go, but the diviners have to carry this out in cooperation with the spirit of the person and the permission of the family. It is assumed that this person left this final decision of when to give up the spirit to the family to help him. But his will is also clear that he would like them to let him go at that moment. Some people bring such bags down themselves because they know their family will not carry out such instructions out of fear of being judged as the one who killed that person or gave orders to kill him. Such judgement might be the spirit judgement if the family went to inquire who killed the person. Such family member will be marked as a person with blood in his hand in the spiritual realm. The spirit judges differently than human beings. African do not give such permission because of the fear of being guilty of bloody hand.

In the real sense, Africans do not partake in whatever seems like giving the order to end the life of someone still breathing or showing signs of life. The issue of Euthanasia is unthinkable to an African. Only God or Deities have such a final decision on life ending. Partaking in ending the life of someone who is alive is disobeying God. It may bring a curse on the family and the generations. It may even bring a curse to the community of that person. Even if the community does not know anything about it. Only when the curse takes effect, the diviner will reveal the cause and the community will correct it. In some cases, this kind of curse costs the loss of lives and properties. Life and property might be lost before the family or community finds out that God laid a curse on them. It may be that an innocent person and not the offender's life and properties are lost. This is why it is difficult to understand how God and the Deities think or how spirits think in general. If the person who brought the curse is punished, then it can be understood. The African notion that no one can exist without community is applicable to funeral rites. It is in the community that one gets the strength and possibilities to live and make changes in life.

CHILDREN'S ROLE

When death strucks a person in the community all members of the community have a role to play except children. Children are vulnerable and should be protected and kept away from the spirit of the dead that hover around the dead and the environment. Children should not be directly involved in funeral rites. They are often marked with things like chalk to protect them from the spirit of death. Children are very receptive and that is why they need extra protection. They may respond and go when the spirit of death calls them to come.

Every other adult from maybe the age of fifteen years and up can participate in safer areas. The women's role has already been mentioned. The elders too. The young adults have to carry out the difficult physical work like digging the grave. There are people who can be chosen by the elders among the young adults to carry out such work. These are young adults who have the spiritual maturity to do that. Digging the grave also involves a certain ritual. Those who carry out the activity have to undergo the ritual. There are a lot of beliefs behind this act. The grave is the final resting place for the deceased. Some deceased would like to have someone with them in the grave so that he is not alone. We have to consider the concept of community relatedness. Being alone in the grave is fearful. Another issue is people who achieved a certain high position in the community like kings should be accompanied by servants in the grave. Some ethnic groups still practice this act. The number of servants may vary in number. It can be dozens of heads of people. It all depends on what the position of that person is and what the elders agreed on. The person cannot be buried until such a number of heads of servants are collected. This is assumed important for the ancestor's role the person will continue to carry out.

In relation to the digging of the grave, the person who digs the grave might die before the burial or shortly after because the deceased may keep the person's spirit in the grave to stay with him. Those with the deceased in the grave have the same fate. He may not let them climb out. Physically they climbed out, but their spirit is held in the grave. In this case, they may soon die suddenly. Such a mistake of losing life is termed a careless death. The community has to take precautions to prevent such mistakes.

The youth carry out a lot of errands to make sure all activities involved within their responsibilities are well done. Most physical activities that need strength to carry out are the task of youth both male and female.

ELDERS

The task that involves wisdom and knowledge are left for the elders, both male and female. Also, security tasks of spiritual protection and measures that should be taken to prevent mistakes and ill will both for the living and the dead are left for the elders. Adults in general take together the responsibility of catering to the well-being of the family and diffusing the strong emotional and mental effects of the loss of life in the family. This often involves activities both on social and spiritual dimensions. These activities can go on for one year. In this period the family is often exempt from many compulsory activities in the community. They need time to close the gap created by death. They also need the time to find a new way to relate with the loved one who is departed to the ancestors. Because in Africa you can never prepare for death. It is only when it happens that you start dealing with it. It does not end with burial rites.

Some issues are settled both spiritually and culturally after the burial. There are consultations by diviners to find out if the burial went as it was supposed to go, and if the deceased is accepted by the ancestors. If such is the case, the family can go on with other issues to deal with. If it is not the case, they will find out and do what is needed to accomplish the goal of union with the ancestors' community. Only if it is something they can do. In case it is not something they can accomplish, then they have to find out what the ancestors want them to do. It may be that they have to isolate the person from their family life too.

All this is done within the first year of the deceased to avoid being late for certain needful actions. Being late for activities means that somebody might be ill or die for not doing certain things in time. In the one year of bereavement and grief, the family receives visitors to comfort them and find out what their needs may be. Simple examples are that if a married couple lost a partner by death, the one who is alive should not marry within that one year of bereavement. In that one year, the partner will need some people who care for her to be in contact. This will help to talk about feelings and so on. It will also help to have support in the case of spiritual, economical, emotional, mental, and social needs, and so on. The remaining partner also needs the protection of the family because someone who lost a partner can be not only vulnerable but weak. It is also the period to make time for people who are coming to pay their condolences and respect to the deceased. Those people need to have the opportunity to show this. The family has to create the space for this.

After one year, it is assumed that the sorrow is over and that the deceased has arrived at their ancestors and settled in their new community and family. The living could pick up life activities again. They will continue all life activities without restraint. The year is marked with ceremonies and rites. Sometimes some rituals are done that focus attention on the complete separation of the physical realm. This means, whether the deceased person finds rest or not, it should not interfere in a negative way with family issues. He should not interfere as if he is alive and belongs to the physical family. Things like being present in the house and so on should be over in one year. Such is no more accepted. But before one year, he will be given the time to get used to crossing over to his ancestors. All family members will work on themselves to see if they are the ones who keep him around.

Grieving continues after one year because the pain of the loss needs time to wear out. One should not force it or hasten it. It should be given the time to erode from the heart and soul and body. Forcing it has a spiritual consequence. It is like aborting something by force which often has repercussions. In case of aborting grief, the person may end up drinking alcohol or even getting a mental problem. Most of the social aspects of grieving are to work on wearing the shock and the heavy emotions out. It is the community's responsibility to work on this together. The wearing out of the effect of death is done in the whole community so that no one will revitalize it later. Everyone is at the same level of getting over it, maybe except the direct family who feels more impact of the death. The grieving together shows also that someone impacted the lives of others in the community. No one lives or dies for himself alone. A person lives and dies in relation to others.

Chapter 19

NATURALIZATION
MENTAL DAMAGE

INTEGRATION MENTAL DISORDER

This story is related to integration. Therefore, I caption it integration mental disorder. I use this story to show what cultural integration can cause on migrants.

A STORY

After my pillow was wetted with tears for three consecutive nights in a row, I realized that I was in trouble. As far as I can remember, it was the first and last time I wetted my pillow with tears. I was deeply in sorrow and deeply troubled. I felt somehow confused. I felt disappointed. The tears came out of worry. I was worried that something negative had happened to me. I did not know what it is. What was clear to me was that I am somehow lost. I had no clue what had happened to me and what I should do. The worry turned to fear. The fear turned to confusion, which turned to agony. It happened more than twenty-five years ago. I still remember it as if it were yesterday. I was less than three years in the Netherlands. I was living in a convent with students and nuns. It was my fourth accommodation of living with Dutch origins in a community house. I was subjected to intensive course for Dutch language and spirituality of Dutch people. The reason for the language is clear and understandable. I have to learn the language so that I can be able to communicate with the Dutch people. Language being one of the components of culture, I made it my primary criteria to learn it. Language is the access to understanding the culture.

Spirituality provides access to why people in that particular culture do what they do and reject what they do not do. It is access to their world view. It was necessary for me to learn why a Dutch person goes to bed and why he wakes up. The issue of rituals was daily exercise as part of my study and formation to be able to work for Dutch origins. I was told that when I started dreaming in Dutch language, then I can be sure that the language and all the trainings are having effect. At least every week, I had to answer the question if I am dreaming in Dutch. I had to minimize being in places where I cannot speak Dutch. My socialization was only with the Dutch community. My friends were Dutch. In short, Dutch was my whole life. I was well occupied with activities around Dutch origins. This was necessary for my study. My study was meant to give spiritual care to Dutch origins and not to migrants. Learning the language, the culture, and understanding Dutch people was the basic condition to do the work. To archive the result of the intensive course, I had to live in the same house with Dutch people. Occasionally, it is in a monastery or convent. In some other situations, I had to live with Dutch students. The purpose is that when I see and interact with mainly Dutch people, eat Dutch, speak Dutch, socialize Dutch and avoid my original culture, then I will easily assimilate and adapt to Dutch culture. This will easily fulfil the requirement of integration in Dutch society. Such intensive form of learning will make me dream in Dutch and make enculturation easily.

SCHOOL SEMINAR

In my third year of living and learning the Dutch life for integration, I was asked by my school seminar organizer to give a workshop at school on African spirituality. The theme of the seminar was spirituality. Many lecturers were also giving workshops on themes relating to spirituality. I was the only African at that theology and philosophy of life school. Each workshop leader had to write a short article for the school magazine. The article explains what the workshop is all about and what people can expect. The school magazine was a special publication for the seminar. I had to write a short article like other workshop leaders.

I had to prepare for the workshop. When I wanted to write things down on African spirituality, I could not remember anything African. The first few weeks I thought maybe I need some time to rest and think. After many attempts, I did not get anything on paper. While the deadline to submit the article was getting close, I became nervous.

It took me time to realize that I had forgotten everything I knew about African culture and spirituality. I could not access the information in me. After wetting my pillow for three nights, I realized that I need help. I went to an African man who sells African arts by central station, Amsterdam. When I came into his shop and explained my problem, he sympathized with me. He comforted me and told me that he receives numerous African students with the same problem of forgetting African culture and spirituality. He went through the same experience while studying economics at one of the universities in the Netherlands. He took time to bring African spirituality to be present in me. He reminded me how we think and act in Africa. He happened to come from the same tribe as me. We could easily connect to our tribal cosmology.

While he was lecturing me by pointing out some arts in his shop, explaining what it symbolizes, my memories came back. I remembered them all. It was as if the door to the African world was opened in me. I could come in it again. I felt joyful and connected again. I became peaceful. The stress and sorrow left me on the spot. It was like being in a presence that makes me feel complete and whole. All this happened in less than two hours. In between, customers were coming in, and he was selling his goods. He gave me some literature and arts magazine to take with me and read. I went home that day and prepared my workshop on African spirituality. It did not take me three hours to write the article and prepare my workshop. The workshop went very well, more than I expected. I did not want to go through the experience of forgetting my culture that cultured my life. I decided to write my master's thesis on African spirituality. It was a joyful journey researching and writing the thesis. It gave me a feeling of being fulfilled in life.

LIVING IN BETWEEN

My life during the integration intensive course was living in between Dutch and African culture. I did not belong anywhere. I was not at home and surely not at ease. My soul was subjected under pressure. I realized that I was often sick. I was vulnerable to seasonal health issues like flu and so on. I was restless. My faith in god was my strength, anchor, and source of joy. Most of my seasonal health complaints stopped after reconnecting with my African culture that year. My immunity became stronger. It also affected my thinking and processing of information. I could objectively and consciously but critically process information from both sides of the culture. The stress in learning and pressure to understand things happening around me was reduced. I was no longer intensively immersed in Dutch culture as a form of learning. I could easily shut information out and chose how to let it in. Although, I had only one intensive assignment, namely to do my study, learn and speak Dutch. Language being the gate to the soul of the people, I had to know why they say what they say and do what they do. Not only that, but I also had to know why they do not say the things they do not say. I had to figure out the answer why they do not say what they mean. Furthermore, important was for me to know why they say what they do not mean.

All interactions were a learning moment for me. Even relaxing and socializing moments were intensive Dutch culture course. After the workshop during the seminar, the main change was that my soul became more protective in the intensity of learning the culture.

MENTAL EFFECT OF INTEGRATION

African people who spoke with me on their integration process shared a similar experience of losing themselves and their identity. During my training and counselling work that led to the writing of this book, I came across many cases of mental problems associated with integration. Their stories are striking. I bundle them together in a kind of summary; otherwise this book will be too bulgy if I write their personal stories one after the other. What is very similar is the issue of identity and personal image distortion. They lost whom they are by violently learning and accumulating thought patterns and ideas which contradict what they know and whom they are. In numerous instances, some did not only lose their personal dignity as human beings, they also project other Africans as very low in personal dignity. They did not do this consciously. It was an unchecked process that took place in them. Losing their identity and dignity, but also projecting this to other Africans, affected the upbringing of their children.

Their children suffer the same experience. You can only give what you have. Their children consciously accumulate such image of those parents in upbringing. This kind of learning goes through senses, which is not rational. Some children want to avoid seeing their parents or such parent with African root at school. They do not want people to know that he or she has African parents or in cases of mixed marriage their African parent. Some did not want the African parent to come and pick him or her up from school. They were ashamed and shy away from their parents. Their parents gave them such low value and dignity.

I have seen many parents from Dutch origin offering excuses to their children for having African parent which gave them the inferiority mark for life. They affirm that they cannot change the situation anymore. This has psychological effect on the children. The child will strive to do something or experience something that will uplift his or her dignity in the other to be proud. Such psychological torture and inner conflict are difficult to understand for someone who does not have the migrant background. It is therefore difficult to treat by someone who does not understand what it is all about. As long as there is no scientific medical information available for such cases, it will become a generational health problem. Each person will transfer it to another generation. This will continue until the chain is broken.

Who they are, are seen as inferior and not good enough. They have to learn the new culture in order to be somebody in the new culture. This message came with pressure to do this in a very short time. What they knew before they came and being content in who they are was simply not good or not good enough. They face the loss of the following heritage and content namely:

Their identity

Their cultural background

Their language

Their rituals

Their spirituality

Their food

Their clothing

Their patterns of thinking

All those things that form the image and identity of whom they are becomes a hindrance to their new future they want to build. They have to put their language behind them. They have to learn another language. They have to think and talk and read in the new language. They are expected to do away with their culture that made them who they are and take a new one. This process goes with physical and mental transformations. The transformation is biological. It affects all parts of the individuals being cultivated by his original culture. Such damages caused in the process of cultural transformation can hardly be diagnosed medically. The medical machines in our health institutions are not tested or build for some diagnoses. Therefore, the scientific medicine will not understand or detect the cause of this kind of health issue. Above all, the issue of the mind is not part of scientific medical diagnoses. The cultural aspect of health hazards is not yet recognized. It becomes understandable why migrants' health problems are more than the indigenous people's health hazards.

It was known that during the Covid-19, high percentage of African migrants died. Covid-19 killed most people who have complicated health problems. It therefore exposed that African migrants have untreated health problems which they carry with them. It is untreated because the scientific medicine does not pay attention to medical anthropology. Attention to cultural medicine and health care will help in treatment of more health challenges of African migrants

What they knew before coming to the new country is not relevant anymore. They have to learn new things. Some who are university graduates are told that the university level of thinking is equal to primary education level of thinking here. Most were advised to register themselves as illiterate, which they did. This happens to most asylum seekers. They also have to behave like illiterates and keep their university degrees away. As long as they are registered as illiterate, they are expected to behave like illiterate. But this does not affect their level of understanding. When they come in contact with people with university level, they will understand them very well. In some cases, they have to pretend in order to maintain that they are illiterate. The pretence is sometimes painfully excruciating and psychologically torturing them. This goes in their file and they are treated like that. While their level of understanding is scientifically academic, they were treated like an idiot and non-educated. It pains them a lot and leads to confusion and depression. By some of them it led to bitter hatred towards the

society. Such bitter hatred causes health hazards too. Hatred is a very heavy burden to carry.

Some migrants react by cutting themselves off from such social interactions. Some will prefer to live on social benefits than to work, where he or she will have to deal with co-workers who treat them as illiterate. They want to protect themselves from such psychological agony and torture.

CULTURE LOST

Some who succeeded in fulfilling the integration experience noticed that they lost their culture and lives in longing for something they do not know. Something that seems like it is a memory of another world. Like a memory of one day coming home somewhere. Some of such examples are already mentioned in this book. Mentally, they feel they are not home and longing for home. They could not pinpoint what they are longing for. But they are sure, that they are in the wrong place. A place that does not accommodate them. A place that is not their home. No matter how much they try, it does not work to make it home. Every interaction with the new land tells them that they are not welcome and that they are not home. They are last class citizens. In all areas of social domain, this experience is present to greet them. The cultural barriers make this experience even worse.

The facts that they have done all that is required of them to be part of the new land, and not knowing what else they could do to be accepted, makes them distressed and upset. Some of them live daily in such anxiety.

The stories of these migrants vary from different experiences with almost the same mental outcome.

FORMER ARMY OFFICER

A former high ranking military woman who attended university and got a philosophy degree in her country. She stood her ground in one of the worst military regimes of our time. When it became too hot for her, that she could not secure her family and extended families, she decides to leave the country with them. She arrives in this country and was granted asylum with her whole family. Because she could not speak the language and does not want to make mistakes in her speech, she could not express her mind. She was treated as a weak woman who came from a culture where women need emancipation.

She was treated as an oppressed and ignorant woman. She described her treatment as being treated like a child. This is partly because of the language barrier. She could not speak or was afraid to speak out her mind. It was a torturing experienced for her. She ended up sitting home to prevent more torture in interaction with Dutch social domain. At home, her dignity, and authority for the tens of family members she brought with her remained. In the society she was treated like a child who needed to learn to be an adult, an emancipated independent woman.

PHILOSOPHY DEGREE STUDENT

There are a series of stories from students who run into mental disorders because of integration and how lecturers treated them. I had some of these cases and was able to help some go back to their country. There are many who could not withstand such mental tortures and could not finish their studies. It is not that they do not have the capacity to carry out their study.

The lack of cultural sensitivity by the lecturers made their study an impossible mission. The short period they have to learn the language and culture is not enough.

DUTCH LANGUAGE & CULTURE

The Dutch language and culture is often unknown to some migrants. In their country of origin, they have no or little information about the Netherlands. Lack of information from their country of origin makes the confrontation and the challenge of integration too big for them on arrival. Some migrants never knew anything about the country before they arrive. They are not conversant with the language and never heard anything about it. Compared with English or French or Portuguese, which people might have heard in one way or the other. The Dutch language is not known as such. People who came here do not have pre knowledge of it and therefore the expectation of learning the language and the difficulty involved comes unexpected to them. Dutch culture is open for certain issues, but through interaction with the culture is only possible with Dutch people themselves.

It is assumed that Dutch people are not open to show their culture. Learning a culture is not something one does on the street or at school. It is done by the indigenous people of the culture at their private homes. It is part of the culture that a Dutch does not invite you to his or her home unless the relationship is somehow tight. This is partly what makes it difficult, especially for Africanmigrants, to learn Dutch culture, at least in a safe way that does not cause them mental disorders.

PATIENT AND HIS HOME PRACTITIONER

Uchenna was living in a village. He was the only migrant in the whole village. Uchenna narrated his story of going to the home doctor telling him he has malaria, and the doctor will tell him he has nothing. He should go home and take some milk and sleep. Uchenna narrated that he was seeing dead people coming to him. He was sometimes hallucinating. He realized that it was not only malaria, but also typhoid and malaria combined. He knows that the combination of both is very deadly. He saw countless people die of the combination of both in Africa.

He just came back from Africa a few days before the symptoms and sickness started. He was a student then and just came back from Christmas holiday he spent in Africa. He noticed all symptoms of malaria and typhoid, which he knew from childhood. The high fever that goes with extreme sweat and extreme shivering cold. Both fever and shivering cold exchanges each other in few minutes. His bed will be wet from sweat when the fever is very high. The sweat will wet the bed and add to the cold. While the body is losing much water at high tempo, the blood is also getting dried up. The test in the mouth and all many other symptoms made him become very sure that he is sick and also in danger of death. He went again to the doctor who told him bluntly that he looks like someone who will improve any sports record, and he came to say he has malaria, and he is sick. His health deteriorated quickly. When it became worse, the home doctor was called by other Dutch people who lived with him in the community, to come for a home visit. When the doctor came and spoke with other people in the house, he called an ambulance. But the other people could not wait for an ambulance and took him themselves to the hospital in Haarlem. Because Uchenna spoke of malaria and typhoid, he was brought to the department of tropical health care. The hospital diagnosed him of having malaria, he was admitted for a long time. When Uchenna went to the doctor after being discharged, the doctor was asking him how he knew that he had malaria.

Uchenna did not trust that the doctors here will take care of his health. He travelled to his home country and pleaded to his home doctor there to treat the malaria and typhoid once and for all. He was afraid that he will easily die of health problems that even herbs in his mother's garden can treat easily. He ended up paying three thousand dollars for intensive treatment in the hospital in his home country. The doctor admitted him for two weeks in the hospital and treated the malaria and typhoid with infuse. The doctor promised him that he will eradicate the parasite from the bone marrow, and he will never suffer from both typhoid and malaria anymore. He also said that the medicine he will be using is expensive. They were imported from Russia. Only those who can afford it are being treated with it. When Uchenna came back and gave the invoice to the insurance, they refused to pay him back. They did not believe it was genuine. Uchenna has to pay for his health care while having health insurance. While I am writing this book, Uchenna has never had both anymore for 28 years.

The doctor in the Netherlands did test for the first two years and noticed that it is completely gone out of the bone marrow of Uchenna. The doctor was lost how it can be treated like that. Such experience made Uchenna to trust his cultural healing approach and believing that the doctor from his culture knows certain health crisis better. This example is not spiritual or mental health care. It is an example of medical anthropology.

The story of Uchenna and lack of trust to the medical professionals is based on experience which many migrants share. Some who could not afford it will pay all they have in order to take care of their health. Those who could not afford to pay for their service will remain with the health problem or the after effect of it. They suffer health poverty because they could not afford their health care. Their health insurance did not cover the specific health care they need.

Chapter 20

DISCOURSE

THE PLACE OF CULTURE IN HEALTH CARE

How would the women react in Africa? The women who are working on breaking the taboos could not have had any problem if they were living in Africa. But in a strange land which they cannot understand and who cannot understand them, the breaking of taboos is very challenging and worrisome. The effect it will have on them from society is unknown to them. After all, society never understands them. Society is not helping them. They could not fall deeper than to fall in their resilient position. They hope anyway that whether the discrimination on health care remains intact, they could be supportive of each other in self-reliance. Africans have always been resilient in taking care of their basic needs. Although the new culture promises to take care of all citizens, their experience is not that they are part of the promised policy.

The worldview and the culture, as described in this book, are gifts handed over to them by their ancestors. The ancestors experienced the world and discovered how to handle life affairs to make the best out of life and living. The odds they faced in their journey of life are transformed into wisdom of life. Such wisdom is encrypted in the culture. The culture contains all of them in different components like spirituality, words/language use, dreams, and rituals. What I did not pay attention to under spirituality are food and clothing. I did not find it necessarily needed. It would make this book too voluminous. I also did not pay attention to African arts for the same reason. Food and clothing could be easily substituted with other cultures food and clothing without serious psychological, mental, or spiritual effects. The four components are basic interests both for Africans in Africa and Africans in the diaspora. The four components need extra attention for further work, be it research, dialogue attention, discourse, and so on. It does not matter what it is called, but what matters is more needs to be known about Africans. It is necessary to know more about these areas for the interest of Africans and the new culture where they are residing. As we read in the African culture explained in this book, one person affects the whole community. In such a community the wellbeing of each person matters a lot. Covid 19 shows us that one person contaminated with virus can be a life threatening for a whole community if not taken serious. This shows that what one person carries in his body can be a death sentence for many. Simple things like shaking of hands or hugging one another can lead to health crisis of another and may even means death to another. Each person's health is important for the whole community's wellbeing.

Health professionals should have an interest in knowing and understanding Africans. They have the responsibility of keeping society safe and healthy. They also need to prevent a possible health crisis. Prevention is an important measure of securing the health of the citizens. Covid-19 has proved that prevention can protect health and reduce the loss of lives. Covid also shows that every human being matters and is worthy of being protected in a community to keep all who live there safe. The health problems of Africans should not be something that will be treated as an isolated issue. Health should come out of the isolation Africans are placed in. When they come out of isolation, those suffering health problems within the community will be discovered earlier before it goes to a level that will affect others, their family members, the community, or the whole society.

Scientific research of applying the culture in healing the Africans is also an important measure to take. Healing lies in culture. Culture is a very important part of achieving healing. I need not expand on this need. I think the information in the book is evidence. Each culture has a healing approach unique to it. Food and drinks are important aspects of culture. Such products come from the land. Culture is making a person grow. It is cultivating someone. Cultivating is what you do that connects you to the land. The land gives food and drink. The smells of food and drink can have healing power on someone. It can also cause sickening effects depending on the experience one had with such food or drink. All other aspects of culture as described have an effect on a person. Applying culture in caring for someone is necessary for our scientific era.

The issue of health care that is not covered by insurance is not left out of the discussions that led to this book. Those who were there explained how painful it is for them to use their meager income to pay for health care because there is no other possibility and surely no one took the responsibility to take care of them. In other words, the Africans who are economically excluded have to find a solution to pay for their health care while they pay for insurance. They are in such a position because healthcare professionals do not understand their ill health. It is well known that he who pays decides. The health insurance coverage the Africans pay should be considered. It is not insurance that pays the whole cost. Those African people pay also for their health care. Just because they are not understood by health professionals, it does not mean that they are not sick. There are professionals within their community who can understand them. Their complains are often seen as fabrication and lies. The reason can be that the health professionals do not know what to do because the topic of cultural sensitivity is not part of their education curriculum.

THOSE PROFESSIONALS NEED COMPENSATION TO CARE FOR THEM

The content of this book is focused on Africans. I can be sure that this kind of insight is needed for other cultures in our society too. I am sure we can find interesting things in the cultures that will help build a society where all different cultures can form a community and be at home with each other. With my knowledge of Dutch culture, European culture, and so on, I know that a lot of issues I brought to knowledge in this book about African culture are not unique to African culture. Some are parallel and some are dressed in another form but with the same meaning and purpose. One can speak of good and evil and another one prefers to use good and devil. In essence all cultures are the same but different approaches and method makes them look different. There is nothing I find in African culture and especially spirituality that I did not find in Christian spirituality or religion.

I use the word spirituality and religion together because most of the world religions like Christianity came first into existence as one person spirituality. In the case of Christianity, it is the spirituality of Jesus Christ of Nazareth. This is applicable to some other world religions. Those religions are often integrated in the culture that accepts them or where they find followers. In some cases, the original culture of that spirituality which becomes a religion will intimidate and dominate the culture of their followers. This is not the case with African Religion which has no founder and does not evangelize or appeal to people to follow it. You are either born in it or you do not have it in you.

Describing the fear that Africans have for the shrine and deities who can kill without discussion. As a Christian, I read how the apostle Peter spoke to Ananias and Saphira about their lies. Peter accused them of testing the Holy Spirit. Both husband and wife dropped dead before him while he was speaking. Peter did not touch them or kill them but the Holy Spirit they lied against killed them. Peter, therefore, is serving the Holy Spirit and because of that, he possesses supernatural power given by God. Such action of killing somebody like that brought fear into the Christian community of the time. They feared the apostle Peter for that.

This is written in the Acts of the Apostles chapter 5 verses 1-11. The fear of lying has this effect before the spirit in some spiritualities and religions. I did not see anything strange in African culture fearing such power that can kill instantly. I am not romanticizing African culture. I am also not criticizing it. As a matter of fact, there is no world culture I can romanticize. When I criticize, it has to do with the falsehood and evil in that culture which destroys humans without any measure to improve it. Lies and falsehood are dangerous and deadly, while truth is redemptive and life. Personally, I think all human beings have to transfigure to another culture. To criticize a culture, one has to look back to that culture and understand how it comes to existence, and then one can criticize the birth of the culture. It is a difficult task anyway, but not impossible. When I criticized the racism culture, I looked back at how it was born, cared for, and upheld. Seeing the effect of it, then I criticized it. This criticism is done from the point of view of mental damage and the further effects it has on the African community. Although racism is not only against Africans.

MENTAL WELL-BEING TRAINING

While I was educating them on mental health and spiritual care, they were receptive and asked questions. They were also sharing experiences that caused mental disorders.These experiences ranged from cultural issues in Africa which they had to live through as described in this book, to experiences in the new culture they are currently living in. The present experiences in the new culture have a great impact on their mental well-being and lifestyle. It ranges from the stereotypical images created about them before their arrival. Such images that are so negative do not allow them to break the barrier. The result of discrimination goes with the image whereby they experience isolation and exclusion in all dimensions of life. This includes the physical dimension, social dimension, economic dimension, psychological dimension, cultural dimension, the spiritual and mental dimension, and so on. This discrimination has a far-reaching effect. The effort to understand and join the new culture and to participate is therefore an impossible task. Only when one is accepted can one integrate and participate. When the door is shut against one, it is not possible to be part of what is happening inside the door. The image of Africans is so inferior that it makes respect for Africans to be nonexistent. Without respect, someone cannot be allowed to be part of the game. One must have something to contribute to be allowed to be part of what's happening.

The low image is a hindrance for society to even find an African as being worthy of the time given to him. The image makes it difficult to invest in Africans. Investment is what one does to something that has value. Especially in a materialistic culture and society, where materials in many cases are valued above human life, Africans have a meager possibility of getting attention. The image puts Africans in a situation whereby all the mentioned dimensions become a barrier they cannot break. The issue of health problems both physical and mental is the assured outcome.

The African history of slavery, colonization, and economic exploitation which the society is grappling with, including all discussions about the historical aspects and actuality doesn't make the already present health problems better. Especially when Africans are kept from receiving the right health treatment. Most of the mentioned issues came across in the gatherings that led to this book. It is a choice I made to keep away most of the issues that Africans experience as part of the major causes of their ill health. It already starts with the encounter of the two worldviews in Africa during slavery, colonial and material exploitation.

The history of such made Africans live in other continents like Europe, South America, and North America forming their own community outside Africa. Such actuality is not a historical past, but a present life experience. Those Africans living on that continent for a long time are still longing to go back home. The notion of being homesick, and going back to Africa shows that mentally, they still see Africa as their home. Africans are very easily adaptive to other cultures. They are receptive to others and accommodative to others. The fact that they, after centuries of living in another continent, still see Africa as the home where they want to go back to says something on a mental level, and the failure to find a community in those continents, they helped in building up economically and otherwise. But they still say, "I wish I was home; I wish was in Africa."

My purpose in educating the Africans was to let them educate others. I know there is a taboo within the community in talking about mental and spiritual health. They realized that they are suffering from it, but they are not talking about it. After the training ended, they refused to go to an unknown group to talk about mental education. I tried to find out why none of them wanted to do that. A lot of those involved were highly educated and have responsible positions in companies and organizations. Some are directors and managers and doctors. The majority are community leaders. Highly educated and responsible pastors and honorable role models of the community were involved. Those were my targets. I assumed that they will be able to grasp the need for mental education and will educate Africans. The group was a mix of males and females, but also youths were involved.

WOMEN GROUP

Another group of professionals and resilient powerful women got the same training in a separate group. One group was taught in the Dutch language and the other was taught in English. Both groups did not know each other. They never met each other. I was the only link to both. What baffled me was that both reacted the same during and after the training. The insightfulness and desire to learn more including discovering the personal interest in using the training for self, family and community support were expressed by both. In both groups are mix of people from the African diaspora first generation and second generation but also people with African roots from South America and other continents who were born there and have never been to Africa. Their root in South America goes back to hundreds of years. But there was no difference in the way they all reacted. It woke my interest in trying to find out why African roots reacted like this to spiritual and to mental health. I also found out that they reacted the same when discussing health problems in general.

One of the things that was common to them is that they want to give this education on health within the community they belong to and trust. It was when they started doing it in those communities, that I realized why they were not keen to do this education in the presence of unknown people in public.

THE WORD TRUST IS VERY IMPORTANT

This request was granted by me. They did not only give education on what happens, but the tips they offer on how to avoid getting mental and spiritual problems were elaborated on in depth. There are also things I decided not to share in this book because it is too much information that will be treated confidentially in the group. Those who were causing mental problems to others were there. Those who were victims explained the hell they went through and how their lives and families were ruined. When I listened to the openness and true kind of confession they authentically expressed in sharing, then I realized why they find it difficult to share this in public with strangers. This is another case than the known case of fearing the spirit or the actor who sometimes remains unknown and wants to hear the result of his evil action on the victim. If the victim reports how he is suffering and the actor fears being exposed, he can decide to end the life of the victim quickly in another method. The last fear was that society seeks every chance they have to take away their children. For this last reason, they urged me to keep them confidential but to share their situation with society.

THE SOUL CALLS

In my former two books namely MIJN DROOM, opzoek naar een rechtvaardige en vreedzame samenleving and HET TRIBUNAL VAN DIVERSITY, DE BIECHT VAN EEN FAMILY GEHEIM, I mentioned the problems Africans face in diaspora because of their skin color. It is unfortunate that their skin color causes other fellow human beings to treat them meanly. This causes not only physical, psychological, mental, and spiritual pains and disorders but also all kinds of health hazards and blocking their emancipation and flows. Many people still have yet to accept them as human beings or full human beings.

The continuous struggle for the continent to be free from colonial rules which were imposed at all levels including political, religious, cultural, economic and all aspects of their existence portrays the image one has about them. The image of people who do not have willpower but can be dominated and made slaves out of them. The racial discrimination and injustice they face because of that at all levels of human existence both in Africa and outside Africa is still a daily reality.

In the issue of slavery, they were bought and sold as livestock, the majority of them were taken out of Africa without any payment. The education materials produced by scholars to uphold all the mentioned issues in order to maintain the status quo of Africa in those images remain evident to transfer this to unborn generations against Africans.

When I got the call for help from the group of Africans my mind raced to all of the above asking the question, how long shall this continue? My effort to bring this to understanding Africans is based on my hope to have a discourse that will bring healing both to Africans as black people and to this new culture Africans need to make a new home. I also hope that the discourse will include other world citizens. My effort in this book to portray the soul of an African through the culture is an effort to request understanding. Africans can be different as they are, but they have a culture that has sustained them. They are human beings with human culture. A culture that was given to them by their ancestors to cultivate them into being human. Their God is the God of their ancestors who gives them the directives to cultivate the culture of living into being human. A human being is born, and being human is cultivated.

COME AND HELP US

Half of my life I lived with Africans and half with Europeans. Some of my European friends asked me why I write against racism after knowing what I know that it is normal for people to think like that. It is a culture that is very deep in the psyche and is impossible to remove or change. This was a discovery some people who went with me on a journey of mental change discovered with shock. They could not believe that it was a culture in which no one is free. You are brought up to think and behave like that. To those friends, I had an answer.

My answer to them is that in my first 25 years in Europe living with Europeans, I was learning. I learned for 20 years to understand them. That was why I was indifferent to the negative biases. When the groups of Europeans with me speak about black people or my country of birth, I assume it has nothing to do with me because there are hundreds of millions and billions of people. I pay no attention. When they speak with negative images of black men, I do not pay attention because it is not about me. After all my color is not black.

When they spoke about me, I tried to explain things for them to understand thinking it would make a difference. But when their negative biases are used to condemn me even without knowing me, just based on my color and African roots, then I noticed that I am already generally condemned because of the negative images. I was indifferent in the past. When I discovered that I was supposed to speak for myself, then I decided to speak for myself. While I spoke for myself, the arguments they brought forward had nothing to do with me personally but with the image of the continent I came from. It was then I understand that those other black men and black people were me. I realized the power of culture.

That is why I started writing and sharing to express the ugly faces of wickedness in cultures. Being indifferent to the wicked biases of others is being indifferent toward yourself. It is being indifferent towards your community and society. It is being indifferent toward human beings. It is inflaming wickedness that has no borders. One day you will surely get your turn. It is a natural law that never fails. Wickedness is like a ground that never gets satisfied with what you give, it will consume it and keep quitting but always seeking more. It never has enough.

This is why I am also writing this book. Those women are my mother, sister, wife, daughter, and family. The men who could not speak are me too. They are my father, brother, and comrade. Their partners and families are mine. Their children are our future leaders and workers in the community. What affects them will affect me directly or indirectly. We are all connected. This is the consciousness we need to build together a community that is healthy and home for all. Such a community is needed more than ever by human beings.

Come and help us is a call we all are supposed to respond to because it is a soul that calls. Everybody has such a calling once in a while in a lifetime. Come and help me or us. The culture that is built in the community uses help us. The individual culture uses help me. My need to respond quickly is based on my knowledge of the African community in society. It is a known fact that they are often materially the poorest of the poor in any society when they are outside of Africa.

THE POSITION OF THESE
WOMEN IN THEIR NEW SOCIETY

The single mothers with young children are materially the poorest of the poor in society. They have a scarcity of every basic material thing for life and living. They have in abundance every kind of problem that can weigh even the strongest person down. They are socially and economically isolated. Health and well-being are luxuries they cannot afford. When or if they receive from the left, it is taken back from the right. They are administratively tortured and intimidated. Judicially they are humiliated and abused. When they asked for help instead of receiving it, they are punished for asking. When their heart is broken and their mind starts freaking out, their only light and hope in life, mainly, their children, are taken from them. Some become like a predator in an effort to see their children at school or at the playground or when the new owner takes the child from school. It is assumed they are not good enough. Their contact with their children means having more uncivilized imbecile people brought up in civilized society.

That they do not fit into society is the often-heard assumption behind closed doors. They bring the quality of civilization down with their presence. Anything that can be used against them is orchestrated. Both verbal violence and any possible form of duress are applied. The general conclusion beforehand is that they are not good for their children. The more they are excluded from bringing their children up, just to prevent them from transferring the uncivilized African culture into their children, the better it is for society to have a child with a higher upbringing. Therefore, any opportunity and reason to deprive them of their children's upbringing are welcome. In the last decade, I have prevented scores of them from committing suicide. Some hundreds fled the country to another country, continent, or back to Africa.

Come and help us. They do not understand us here. Come and help us, they hate us.

The voice did not stop echoing in my mind, even though my agenda was full, I knew there was no one else they can turn to. I have seen their suffering and their world. I have heard their stories in many different dimensions, conditions, and places. I know their reality and their fear for the future of their children. I know their poverty. I also know their strength. I know them. I went to them.

PRISON

I have seen a woman who brought her children up as a single mother. She had no regular income. It was very difficult for her. She could not build a pension to live on in her old age. She came to me to borrow money to get a lawyer. Her daughter who is a single mother was sent to prison for many years and she has to take care of her grandchildren. At the same time, she has two adult children of her own, a man and a woman over 50 still living with her in her house. These two children cannot take care of themselves because of health issues. She has no room for her grandchildren. Her hope was to get a lawyer who could maybe appeal the case to get her daughter out or reduce the number of years. This would alleviate her suffering of long traveling hours daily to take care of her grandchildren in another city. This woman is highly advanced in years. She narrated why she could not get permanent work to build her pension. I asked why somebody should suffer so much. I thank God I was able to support them to get her daughter out of prison. The aged woman could be alleviated from the care of her grandchildren.

COURT

I once saw a woman in the court who took off her clothes to show the female judge her cesarean section as a life mark and narrated the pain of delivering her third child. She asked the judge to be lenient with her and not take her third baby away as she did with the other two. This was her desperate attempt to show her pain to the judge. The company that had already seen the opportunity for more income in her baby won the case. She needed the community to support her in the court hearing, but this time scores of African women gathered to take care of the child to make sure the child was brought up in African culture. The judge later accepted it and released the child, but later on, the judge took the child again.

This has been the new normal custom for African families. Mothers' hearts and souls are wounded. Their mind freaks out. Children are disoriented and face cultureless upbringing. Mothers dream of their children being taken away. Some of the children are kidnapped from school or childcare as the mothers describe it.

A child is the future and destiny of an African woman. She gives all the best of her life energy to the child. A child is formed with her blood and water, they are nurtured with her life energy and washed with her blood by birth. When she asks for help, she is punished. Their life is often spent in fear that they will lose their child one day. This is a shocking culture for them. It is something they cannot imagine in African culture.

One may ask, why doesn't she ask for help? It is because she will be punished. In many cases, she is condemned as an unworthy mother, and a criminal, and she is treated as such. What I am describing is an extra issue that the group of women faces next to other biases and difficulties.What happens to these minds? They need at least basic mental support.

THE RESILIENT SPIRIT OF A BLACK WOMAN

African people have always managed a difficult history. I need not mention the long list of difficult history in dealing with non-Africans and also natural issues in Africa. The spirituality and ethics as explained shows why they can manage such a difficult history. The spirituality of resistance is a strength inherited from the ancestors. Resilience, as the women in this society show in this book, is part of such inheritance. Africans have carried this spirituality and morals with them wherever they are in any part of the world. They always withstand the test of time which is the toughest test in nature. The test of time is the toughest test in creation. Anything that is out of time has an everlasting existence. Nothing inside time can last the test. As we can see in the culture, the source of life is God. God is the source and secret of life. Africans focus all their being on the hands of God. In the test of time, they hope to the last minute that God shall take care. It doesn't matter how the condition may be, God has the final word. It is often in Africans that you can see the deep-rooted spirit of resilience. Because even when they lack everything, their resilience becomes clear.

When everything is lost, that's when you see what someone's source is like. The source is very vital to know the truth about somebody. Africans find peace and strength in their spirituality. Their emotions and senses and body are often their instrument to dance and sing for hours and days. They do not need any musical instruments to do that. Clapping of hands is very common as a musical instrument. The creativity to evoke joy and happiness is endless. Dancing and singing are hospital treatments for mental, psychological, spiritual, and physical disorders. It heals their traumas. It heals their emotional breakdown. It prevents a lot of possible health breakdowns. This is a culturally given healing method transferred from the ancestors. Their body is the house in which they actually live. The body is like a hospital building with all the healing equipment in it. The surrounding nature is the medicinal world with all elements for ritual and healing. This also includes visible and invisible healers.

This treatment gives them access to joy and positive energy and leads them in doing good things for themselves and others. It raises and maintains positive power in them.

Very deep inside their soul is an amazing reservoir of spiritual power. One has to fall so deep to the bottom of his existence, to discover there is no other place to land than in the hands of God. That is the deepest one can fall. It is amazing to land in the deep darkness into a hand that receives you with ultimate love and peace. This does not only convince one to believe in God, but it makes one trust in God. This is why Africans have incurable trust in God. Such trust releases power. A power with its source in God. Power flows from the wealthiest source of its origin. A power that the world cannot give. That no man can take. That wickedness cannot reach or destroy. A power hidden so deep and secured to withstand the time of wickedness. The inexhaustible power from an inexhaustible source. When all the world can give is taken away, such as basic material life sustainability, or when human value is deprived, or when the human being has degenerated, this power shines in the form of resilience like a light shining bright in thick darkness.

Resilience becomes more visible. The source says it all. The source of goodness. The source of justice. The source of truth. The source of righteousness. These virtues are not from the world. That is why it is not in the world cultures. This is why you often stand alone when you stand for any of those virtues. The notion that truth will set you free is not the human culture. Those who tell the truth are often on the run. That is the terrible truth about the truth. When you stand for the truth, you often stand alone. This is why lies reign and are protected. Lies are the governing culture of the world.

Coming from a culture where lies mean death into a culture where truth means death or punishment is challenging. It is also confusing. One loses trust when the environment is full of deceit and bias. Living with the fear of lying in a culture of lies because you come from a culture where lies mean death is stressful and confusing.

Swearing in a book, in the name of God, or a declaration in form of an oath, does not have a direct effect on people. All this is applied to make people say the truth. I was wondering why people do not mean what they say and do not say what they mean. The terrible truth about the truth taught me why Africa seeks the truth by the spirit and not in the oath without direct consequences. In the new culture, they bear in mind that the deities and ancestors' spirits are monitoring them and above all God is watching them. They fear not only human beings but the spirit who sees and hears them in all situations. This aspect of culture is part of the source of cultural stress that affects mental well-being. The mind suffers both information management from the former culture and system of justice and the new culture system of justice. Human beings are in charge of justice in the new culture and the spirit is in charge of justice in the former culture. I wanted to point out this difference which has a big impact on their mental well-being.

MENTAL WELL-BEING AND MIND

Taking into consideration the difficult history of Africans including all forms of dehumanization in their new culture and the effect it has on their mind, we design a cultural approach to work in our mind. Concerning the issue of mind, Africans in their community life pattern and attitude have their own approach to keeping the mind healthy. I will not elaborate on their approach in this writing. The African's aim is to keep the mind healthy. The mind as we know it is a complex organ with lots of activities at the same time. It needs to be checked. African community life habits act as a mirror to each other in the community. In community interaction, Africans are very conscious of each other's thinking faculty.

The way you present issues, use words, and all issues involving the thinking faculty are observed by the community. They know that each person in the community has a pattern of thinking. Observation is extremely important in leadership and representation issues. This is how they select people who are rhetorically well-gifted and those who are wise. In any kind of leadership, be it in the talent of singing, dancing, crafts, teaching, healing, and so on, the mind of the person is considered. There is also leadership by merit, agreement, or by right of birth.

An agreement can be in the form of a rotating leadership. In this form, someone in the community can be chosen to take over the leadership when it is the turn of that community. Leadership by merit is when a family is given a certain kind of leadership role which remains from generation to generation. Leadership by birth is like the permanent role of the firstborn in the family which no one can compete with or try to take over as long the firstborn is alive. In any of the mentioned leadership tasks, the mind of the person is not overlooked. When the mind is assumed to not be healthy enough, someone who has a healthy mind can be asked to assist them. The person with the healthy mind can represent that person in difficult issues that are challenging to the mind.

The community knows whose mind is beautiful, whose mind is different from others, and whose mind is freaking out or sick. In speaking and acting, such things are exposed. They take notice of this in time and find out what to do for those who are losing their mind or those who have lost it already. They take the necessary measures for this. They know the impact a crazy mind can have on the community.

Africans see the mind as a funny faculty and sometimes deceiving to the person. It hardly lets the person know that he is freaking out. The person will always believe that things are well with him. That is the community's role to observe this themselves and act on it.

In their diagnoses to help someone who has lost his mind, both social and spiritual measures are applied. The social measures are often done preventively. Like when someone dies, the community's general grieving has the effect to prevent someone from feeling lonely and thinking too many negative things which will derange the mind. Preventive measures, like sharing the pain together, take away the feeling of loneliness. Making jokes and laughing together, including all other activities that exchange pain and joy are meant to alleviate the mind of the pain. Africans believe that when someone is subjected to long-term durable pain and suffering, the mind will not function properly. It may need a long time to reset it again. Let me now separate the healthy mind and malfunctioning mind from an African perception.

HEALTHY MIND

Africans understand fully well that someone can be harsh to you and act negatively. Someone can say things that lift you up, bring you down, or make you feel bad. Your healthy mind does not let you keep on repeating those painful experiences after it has been said and done. Repeating such things will imprint such pain in your mind and thereby programming it to become a sick mind. That is why they find a way to get rid of it. Expressing feelings fully is an approach to reduce the power of such negative utterances against you.

Everyday life is challenging enough for living. Your healthy mind helps you to go about in your life looking at the beautiful side of things for you. It helps you see the positive attributes of your life. It does things like keeping the good memories above the painful ones. In some cases, it tries to shut the painful experiences down. It does this to prevent such experiences from running your life into perpetual suffering. The community is aware that they are going to be part of your eternal suffering if it is not curtailed. They also know that such suffering shall not end there but goes from generation to generation. Such generational suffering brought into the community by one mind is what the community wants to prevent. The community wants to remain strong and safe.

Your healthy mind does not allow you to be jealous when you see the success and great achievements of others. It does not encourage or allow you to compare yourself with others in a negative way or feel low and down. It helps you to be true to yourself, love yourself, and take good care of yourself by doing the things that help your life to be better than otherwise. In other words, your healthy mind does not allow you to destroy yourself and be addicted to things that are destructive to you. It helps you to make the best of yourself. It reminds you about your uniqueness in the whole creation. Working to give you peace, and joy and keep you in a state of wholeness and satisfaction in life. When you are in that state, it will work to edit more and more of those things that will keep on lifting you into the state of blissfulness. The more you are lifted, the more it will edit to keep you in a state of gentleness, humility, and meekness towards other people so that your temperance will keep you united with others. Your life will be complete.

Your healthy mind knows how to bracket a lot of things around you like anger, hatred, sadness, and all forms of negativities in the name of forbearance and longsuffering till time takes those things away. You will thereby become an overcomer and look forward to good tidings. It protects you by resisting the pull to reduce you to a life of bitterness and disappointment. Such a state of life occurs when you see the success of others and want to be like them. Even when it is clear to you that they made efforts and sacrifices to achieve the success and fortunes they have.

You know the path in their life that brought them fortunes is not for you. Your healthy mind keeps you focused on your own course and life mission. It keeps you compassionate toward yourself. It helps you not to compare yourself and your condition with others who have different upbringings and challenges in life affairs.

Your healthy mind is expectant in moments of despair and conditions of hopelessness. It knows how to hope. It keeps the evidence of grace and kindness, but also beautiful things. It keeps on looking forward to goodness. These moments can be good news from someone or anything positive. It does not matter how long it lasts; it is registered as a beacon of hope for the next.

Your healthy mind is connected and receptive to God, especially with good ideas and fine-tuned intuition. Intuition is receiving some information that does not come from human beings, but from the spiritual world. It is a knowing that nobody could tell you, you just know it without further evidence and further explanation. It just comes into you, and it is true and trustworthy. Things that will bring you into stagnation and setback, help you to let them go. They help you to forgive and keep the past in the past and live fully today and be present in your community.

They help you heal from injuries and pains of the past. It has the intelligence and warning to let you seek help or talk to someone when it is no longer functioning well.

Your healthy mind knows that continuously finding fault with yourself will not benefit you. It protects you from being overruled by fear, and worry, and avoids catastrophic imagination. It, therefore, holds a grip on them so that you can start living. It knows that things can go wrong whenever and wherever they must, but you do not live in fear of it.

A healthy mind can take an intelligent risk with a foreigner or stranger. It has and gives fundamental trust in humanity but maintains a level of suspicion of certain people. It makes sure that life's worst experience is not applied to destroy the possibility of good emerging in a situation. For example, if you have a painful experience of betrayal of trust with someone from a certain country, it does not stand in the way for you to accommodate someone from the same country into your trust circle. Or when you fail at something, it will not allow you to try it again.

A healthy mind refuses to let itself be silenced by all the many sensible arguments in favor of rage and loyalty. They are still long lists to mention, but we can understand the work of the mind with the issues mentioned.

Africans see the mind as an organ with many compartments that can be opened and closed. It chooses then which door is appropriate to open and which door must be tightly shut depending on your particular circumstances. It can shut the door of certain things you did when you are in certain situations. It can shut the door of wild fantasies when you are looking at someone, maybe even a family or community member. It can shut the door to prevent you from thinking of harming yourself with sharp objects or committing suicide. Keeping the flashes of negative thinking rather than fixating on negative things is also a way it keeps you healthy. It has the mastership of censorship to edit and choose the best thing to do. Because our senses bring a lot of information to the mind, it listens well with ultimate concentration and can shut out any other distractions to allow focus. With such concentration, it knows what to shut off and what to allow in. It will organize the information received and give you what to use for your needs. It is your best adviser.

Maybe by looking into some of the features of a healthy mind as I outlined, one can identify what can happen when your mind falls ill or is disturbed. You can acknowledge the extent to which your mind is ill or call it a mental illness which is ultimately just as common and that the mind is an essential body part. For example, when you have a physical problem like broken bones, a sore throat, a disturbing headache, an eye problem or toothache, and so on, you seek help to restore your good health.

When the mind is overstressed with negativities and too many loads for too long, it is bound to break down. Like it happens to the physical body that is overstretched for too long. The body suffers injuries or wounds and needs some time to recover. This also happens to the mind. One can understand why Africans can be resilient. Also, expressing emotions and feelings ultimately can be an elixir for the mind that is bulging to a mental explosion.

Everybody is worthy of love, attention, and sympathy if he needs support for his mind and mental health. Knowing what a healthy mind does and the heavy-duty work the mind does every minute of your life, you can understand that it can be overworked, or things can go wrong with it. You need, therefore, to maintain it well. In African culture, one needs others to see it go wrong or to help maintain it healthy.

MALFUNCTIONING MIND

Let me compare the mind with the stomach. It is a better comparison because the stomach receives and contains our food and drink and digests it and gives us the energy to work and keep us fit. When you eat something that upsets your stomach, you can get stomach pain or diarrhea. You can be sick. In that case, you know something went wrong. You start checking what it may be. You may do one or another thing to get well again. But you pay attention to the stomach and seek healing. Diarrhea is one of the ways the stomach uses to heal itself and keeps you well. Both the pain and diarrhea are means of communication of the stomach to you, that you gave it something it cannot handle. Vomiting is also another way. The stomach works to get rid of that which is not good for your body and health. In some cases, you have no other choice when the stomach decides that you have to get rid of what it rejects. It must go out in any way possible. This is easily understood because it is physical and you can see and feel it. When the mind has collected information that makes it unhealthy then you can see the signs. You can talk about mental diarrhea in this case. It will start malfunctioning. It will not edit very well and cannot process information to keep you healthy. Its censorship is no longer accurate. You can have the following signs, such as tiredness of the mind or mental weakness and vulnerability. You can experience confusion, anxiety, fear, and stress that leads to many other things and depression might also occur.

Anger and hatred, including wrath and furiousness, start occupying space in the mind. Thinking that leads to strife, and envy that leads to murder keeps on increasing without control. All those things keep on multiplying because the mind is no longer censoring and shutting the gates down, one day it will explode, and the thinking will be carried out. Therefore, people act in a way that you can ask yourself, how can someone do such a thing? Those people are not aware of mental diarrhea, and they are not conscious of their minds. In other words, they are not mindful of themselves.

This malfunctioning of the mind is not healthy. It is no longer connected and keeping you healthy. The longer you allow the situation to keep on going the more damage it causes to your health. Such a malfunctioning situation will in the long run become the state of your mind. Your mind will adapt to it. This means your mind is programmed to work in a way that will keep you mentally unhealthy. Knowing that the mind has as much influence as spirit above physical in the African context at least, the whole body will be sick. To some, it becomes a hell that makes them either kill themselves or even kill others. It makes others hold someone hostage or hold someone in order to be tapping from the life of that person to feed his or her unhealthy mind. People around that person do not feel free and safe. They are often afraid and always watch out. They are always alert. It does not matter what the person's position may be. It is unhealthy because it does not only affect the health of that person but also the health of others close and far away. Those under the influence of such a person are sometimes treated as slaves, dominated, manipulated, and intimidated. The person can be openly harmful or subtly harmful to himself and others.

The person may not be aware because the mind is more difficult to understand. This is because you cannot think outside your mind. You need another person to think outside your own thinking. The other person is like a mirror to your mind. In other words, the other person tells you or is a reflection of what your mind is doing. Africans use the community life opportunity to see this in one another and give support before it is too late. You can do the same thing when you have stomach pain or diarrhea. In case of diarrhea, you may prefer to stop eating until your stomach is at peace again.

In the case of your mind, it will help to stop thinking or reduce it, but it is difficult to achieve. Like in diarrhea your stomach is ejecting much more than it normally does. In a malfunctioning mind, your mind is running a marathon with less editing and controls. Such a marathon brings you into a state of stress and your body becomes restless. Your mind can no longer control and shut down damaging information. The barriers and the door are no longer working as it is supposed to work. Your own safety is in danger and the safety of others you might physically or emotionally harm is vulnerable. You are like a car in a high-speed race without a driver or control mechanism approaching someone at the zebra crossing. The person crossing may assume that the car is going to slow down or stop, but they do not know that there is no driver or control in it. Your mind is like the driver and your body is like the car in motion. You normally see the car from a far distance, only when you come close can you see the driver. Your body is visible, but your mind is not. Knowing that someone's mind is malfunctioning is often when either you are verbally or physically hurt or someone else is hurt by the person. Africans curtail such hurt in their community through preventive measures. Any measures that fail to prevent someone from a malfunctioning mind are termed to be caused by a spirit. This implies that the person has done a grievous offense whereby a malfunctioning mind is a severe punishment from the spirit.

Well, the issue of a disturbed or upset mind is the same as an upset stomach. One needs to pay attention to it. You need someone who can help you redeem your mind to its original state of creation or to a healthy mind. The specialist can be a spiritual caregiver who is trained for it. It can be a psychologist or other professionals, but it can also be a family member, friend, or colleague, even a stranger may do very well.

Culturally sensitive care implies that the culture in which you are cultivated is taking these things into consideration and applying it in the healing process. The mind and body accept what they know and what they can handle.

Applying an African culturally sensitive mindset for mental healing, I worked with them on the African approach. Culturally we paid attention to the benefits of a healthy mind and how we maintain it in African culture. It was a reaching out to the inner strength of Africans and revitalizing it. It was months-long training with some of the benefits I shared here. We went through some of the things written in this book. In most cases, I did not need to mention them before they recalled them from their upbringing and community life.

The benefits of a healthy mind that release the women's power to break the taboos is what I tapped into. I saw no other way to liberate them from the mental prison the new culture put them in. It may be out of ignorance that they are in a mental prison. It does not matter how they enter and why they are in there, redemption was my target. We are still in the process, but these things are written to share with others, for the reader. I cannot share the feelings and effects on the participants.

Africans do not need much to be redeemed. They only need to reconnect back to the source. That source is my effort to reconnect people to it. It is also a reconciliation.

A healthy mind is your healthy body. Your healthy body is your basic wealth. Your basic wealth is your life. It does not come without effort.

I make the effort to write this book on request of those who are not heard. Those women calling for help for their family and themselves. I heard them. I am present in their lives. I listened to them. I cared for them. I cared for what they care for. This book is meant to let their voices be heard. When their voices are heard, then they are not alone. They're hope and trust that there are people of good will in the society who can care about their lives and their life course. I wrote this book with hope to start the discourse on this growing health hazards for the migrants that has been neglected all the time. There must have been migrants' health professionals who made this call before. There must be my predecessors who worked to alleviate the health crisis of migrants who searched for healing in their culture of origin. It is important to act now before we face health segregation in public health care. The cultural sensitive care policy is a matter of urgency. It should not wait, especially after Covid-19 exposed all that was known and all that was hidden on the issue of migrant's health. The health professionals cannot afford to fail in providing health policy to improve the health of the migrant people. I did not touch the workload and contributions of migrants in the labor force of the nation. Their health care should be a care for the health service. Their cultural health care deserves what it takes to make it available to them.

What I wrote in this book does not reflect my belief, my mind, or who I am. I observed, attached, and detached. We all suffer together as human beings. We affect one another in community life. Our basic call in life is to live in a community of all human beings. We have a lot to offer to each other. That is why the creator loves diversity and made it. Each person in the creation and each soul has a mission to serve the creation. It does not matter where and how one is born and brought up. Each person is unique to fulfill something no other person on earth could fulfill. Keeping a healthy mind is the assurance of safety for all human beings. That is why I am committed to the work. My contribution is to support each person to fulfill their soul mission.

AFRICANS

Though, Africans can have more than thousands of different languages based on different tribal tongs. They can have uncountable rituals. Their spiritualities may seem as numerous as more than the one billion population of Africans. Each African dream in his or her own way and interpret it in his or her manner and understanding. Their skin color may differ. There is still something that make them to be called Africans. Spiritual thread connects and bind them to a community that puts them together in one. They are things that never dies or be silenced in an African. It is not material which can be left or get lost. It is spiritual. Likewise, it is nonmaterial. It is what make them move. It is what make their feet soul light and easy to move for dance.

Even if their heart is heavy with burdens and pains, their feet remain light. Their body does not need to warm up to be free. Their lips cannot be tied or sealed by anger or emotions in order not to be able to open for laughing or singing. It is a choice which African's make in any situation, either joy or pain, to open his or her mouth and chose to laugh or cry. Both are soothing for the soul and heart, even though they work differently. Their throat can sing, and their tong can make the music. Their lungs are like organ pipes for music instrument. Their body is a complete and perfect biological instrument for music and dance, which brings joy and peace. They do not need man made instrument to make music. Music is soothing for the soul and the heart. When the heart sings, the leg becomes lighter and can be lifted to dance.

Dancing and singing, and other body movements are biological health treatment against trauma, depression, anxiety, stress, and all kinds of spiritual and mental disorders are treated. Their body contains the temple and hospital for their healing. Such activities are for their natural health and wellbeing.

Their hair, skin color, voice, face, how they think and talk, how they walk, their behavior and anything else you can think of about them are spiritually cultured. It is the spiritual soul that makes African share that sameness. It is not relevant if they left the continent some centuries ago and the generations after has never been there. Likewise, it seems to be the only continent where Africans who are not touched by mental slavery calls home. Why is Africa the almost only continent where Africans feel at home? Why do Africans understand each other easily than an outsider?

This is about when you communicate with someone who thinks and communicates holistically while you think and communicate fragmentarily. Africans think in a round or circular manner. In the Netherlands, people culturally think more in a linear and square manner.

Communication between both can lead to psychological or spiritual short circuit because of the difference in philosophy. Misunderstanding each other is easy. African can hardly be part of such community. An African have the need of belonging to a community. That is the need of his or her innermost soul. That is his or her soul journey. African does not know loneliness. Loneliness is a sickness for those who are not part of a community.

This book shows how the women who are often seen as the best army of God in a fierce battle or in cultural change confront the life-threatening taboos Africans are facing.

In this book, I used difference kinds of terms interchangeably to express the same thing almost.

I used SPIRITUAL. Spiritual has to do with the human spirit or soul. It is opposed to material or physical things. It is internal, psychic, invisible, non-material, and psychological pertaining to religion or religious belief. We use the expression of spiritual leader of a nation, spiritual leader of a religion, spiritual leader of a church and so on.

I used Psychology as the scientific study and research of the human mind and its functions. The study to know what influences human behavior in each context but also the study of conscious and unconscious phenomena, including feelings, emotions, and thoughts.

The issues relating to mental characteristics, biological influences, environmental factors, social pressures, and attitudes that affect a person or group.

I used MENTAL, which refers to the mind in relation to disorders of the mind, psychiatric and psychogenic. It involves the intellectual, cerebral, brain, and rational.

The African approach is not conventional. It is not scientific. It is not rational dominated, but senses dominated.

This is not just in health issues. African culture including religion and all aspect of the culture are not scientific. African religion and culture are not written down anywhere for anyone to follow. The health care is not scientific. It is guided by the nature and spiritual realms.

I wish you pleasure and understanding in reading the book. It can be a personal spiritual journey for you to understand more about yourself and the world around you.

ABOUT THE AUTHOR

Godian Ejiogu is a spiritual caregiver and chaplain for African roots in the Netherlands. He specialized in culturally sensitive care for African people. As director of Peace Servant and chairman of Foundation Collectively Strongly Rooted, he educates and guides people living in a culture of health and peace. He lectures in different Theology Universities and high schools and minister at God's Peace Ministry.

www.ingramcontent.com/pod-product-compliance
Lightning Source LLC
LaVergne TN
LVHW041309200726
843509LV00009B/424